FILLED WITH THE
Holy Spirit

FILLED WITH THE
Holy Spirit

By: Fr Kyrillos Farag

ST SHENOUDA PRESS
SYDNEY, AUSTRALIA
2023

FILLED WITH THE HOLY SPIRIT

By: Fr Kyrillos Farag

COPYRIGHT © 2023
St. Shenouda Press

All rights reserved. Except for brief quotations in critical publications or reviews, no part of this book may be reproduced in any manner without prior written permission from the publisher.

ST SHENOUDA PRESS
8419 Putty Rd,
Putty, NSW, 2330
Sydney, Australia

www.stshenoudapress.com

ISBN 13: 978-0-6457703-5-3

All scripture quotations, unless otherwise indicated, are taken from the New King James Version®. Copyright © 1982 by Thomas Nelson, Inc. Used by permission. All rights reserved.

Contents

Introduction	7
The Holy Spirit Will Set You Free	9
The Spirit Helps our Weakness	15
Virtue Through the Treasure of the Spirit	21
The Spirit Covers our Spiritual Nakedness	25
From the Mysteries of the Holy Spirit	31
The Holy Spirit Working in Us	35
Forcing Ourselves to Heed the Spirit Within	41
Be Instructed by the Spirit	47
Renewal in the Spirit	53
The Spirit of Truth	57
Accepting the Fiery Spirit into our Lives	63
The Holy Spirit Renews our Image to be that of Christ's	67
The Holy Spirit is Our Comforter and Advocate	73
The Immense Gifts of the Spirit in our Lives The	77
Bearing the Fruits of the Holy Spirit - Love	83
Bearing the Fruits of the Holy Spirit-Joy	89

Bearing the Fruits of the Holy Spirit- Peace	95
Bearing the Fruits of the Holy Spirit- Longsuffering	101
Bearing theFruits of the Holy Spirit -Kindness	107
Bearing the Fruits of the Holy Spirit- Goodness	113
Bearing the Fruits of the Holy Spirit -Faithfulness	119
Bearing theFruits of the Holy Spirit -Gentleness	125
Bearing the Fruits of the Holy Spirit- Selfcontrol	129
The True Christian is Filled with the Spirit	133
Don't Quench the Holy Spirit	139
Be Filled with the Spirit	145

Introduction

In a world where the divine seems distant and spirituality seems to move at a turtle's pace, "Filled with the Holy Spirit" calls for a profound awakening. Are you yearning to take the first steps to repentance? Are you seeking the Holy Spirit's fire to ignite within? Dive into this spiritual journey where every sin and misstep is an opportunity to invite the Holy Spirit into your life, to lead you towards the path of repentance and growth.

Drawing from the timeless wisdom of St. Macarius the Great, this journey is a tapestry of spiritual contemplations designed to illuminate the transcendent power of the Holy Spirit, and inspire you to invite His presence into your daily life.

In each chapter of "Filled with the Holy Spirit" Fr Kyrillos Farag draws from the teachings of St. Macarius, challenging you to form a deeper, more intimate relationship with God. The book reassures you of the Holy Spirit's support in your battle against bodily temptations and spiritual transgressions. As St. Macarius professes, "These things are obtained gradually, and they require time, effort, patience, and much love and longing for the Lord."

Join us on this transformative journey, allowing the Holy Spirit to guide your prayers, fasting, and vigils, and leading you to taste the sweetness of repentance. Dive into this spiritual journey and allow yourself to be ignited by the fiery Holy Spirit.

The Holy Spirit Will Set You Free

Often we feel that we lack a strong will, are not motivated, cannot pray, do not have joy, do not labour and make no progress in our spiritual life. Essentially: sluggish and burdened. We feel the heaviness of the body's cravings which creates a difficult time and serious challenges in our life.

St. Paul beautifully expressed this common experience: "For the good that I will to do, I do not do; but the evil I will not to do, that I practice" (Romans 7:19). He goes on to say, "But I see another law in my members, warring against the law of my mind, and bringing me into captivity to the law of sin which is in my members. O wretched man that I am! Who will deliver me from this body of death?" (Romans 7:23-24)

Similarly, St. Macarius the Great experienced the same, which he mentions in the second of his fifty homilies. He spoke of the "old man" and the "new man" explaining in detail how Satan caused humankind to fall and how he now dominates our thoughts, feelings, minds and hearts. St. Macarius says, "This is the old man who lives inside us; he is at enmity with God because the person looks with evil eyes, hears with evil ears, has feet which are swift to do evil, hands that work iniquity and a heart which devises evil things".

God promises to set us free from all the evil within us. St. Macarius adds, "It is impossible to separate the soul (the person) from sin unless God should calm and turn back this evil spirit inhabiting both the soul and body." Furthermore, St. Macarius says, "Anyone who watches a bird flying may wish they could fly, yet they cannot fly without wings. Even so, the human will is present to be pure, blameless and spotless, to be always without evil and in communion with God, yet they do not truly have the power." Unfortunately, we do not have the power to achieve this alone. What is the power we need? It is the power of the Holy Spirit which frees us from sin.

Dear reader, do not underestimate the power of the Holy Spirit, but rather strive to recognise His power in your life which as St. Macarius says, has the power to set us free. Wait day and night with hope and ask continuously, unceasingly, and eagerly for the Holy Spirit.

St. Macarius continues his homily "Just like the light of day, there is the divine wind of the Holy Spirit breathing through and refreshing souls who live in the day of the divine light. The divine wind of the Holy Spirit passes through the whole nature of the soul, its thoughts and the substance of the soul and all the members of the body, as it recreates and refreshes them with a divine and ineffable tranquillity." As a result, the soul attains an unspeakable rest, living with all the fruits of the Spirit – which is often missing in our life. For this reason, our Coptic Orthodox Church places great emphasis on the Apostles' Fast.

Consider the meeting between our Lord Jesus Christ and Nicodemus in the Gospel of St. John: "There was a man of the Pharisees named Nicodemus, a ruler of the Jews. This man came to Jesus by night and said to Him, 'Rabbi, we know that You are a teacher come from God; for no one can do these signs that You do unless God is with him.' Jesus answered and said to him, 'Most assuredly, I say to you, unless one is born again, he cannot see the kingdom of God.' Nicodemus said to Him, 'How can a man be born when he is old? Can he enter a second time into his mother's womb and be born?' Jesus answered, 'Most assuredly, I say to you, unless one is born of water and the Spirit, he cannot enter the kingdom of God. That which is born of the flesh is flesh, and that which is born of the Spirit is spirit. Do not marvel that I said to you, 'You must be born again.' The wind blows where it wishes, and you hear the sound of it, but cannot tell where it comes from and where it goes. So is everyone who is born of the Spirit.'" (John 3:1-8).

Jesus' words to Nicodemus resonate with the words of St. Macarius. Indeed, we should be born from water and Spirit. Jesus told Nicodemus that flesh gives birth to flesh, and the Spirit gives birth to spirit. This should not surprise us as these words summarise the Christian life and carry the message of our contemplations in this book. Jesus came to grant filiation to the Spirit, allowing us to appropriate the Spirit's traits; much like children will inherit the traits of their parents. Consider saints such as St. Anthony, St. Macarius and many others, how they seized the traits of the Spirit to lead a spiritual life.

"DO NOT UNDERESTIMATE THE POWER OF THE HOLY SPIRIT. TRY TO RECOGNISE THIS POWER IN YOUR LIFE."

The Apostles were born of the Spirit on the Day of Pentecost and received new traits such as purity, joy, meekness and power. They had no fear, and their old thoughts were altered; they no longer cared about their status but rather submitted to the Holy Spirit. It is this power of the Holy Spirit which can give you and I divine characteristics. Most of us desire to live in purity, peace, meekness and joy but cannot. Why? Because we depend on ourselves without looking for the power of the Holy Spirit in our life.

We initially received the Holy Spirit through the Sacrament of Baptism and Confirmation. The Holy Spirit however does not come to those who have no desire to live with God. The cause of weakness in our life is the absence of the Holy Spirit. This is because we don't give the Holy Spirit a chance to make us holy, enlighten our hearts, eyes and spirits, nor give us the power of a holy life.

The saints eagerly increased the fire of the Holy Spirit through prayer, reading the Bible, receiving Holy Communion and obeying the commandments. They obtained the traits of the Spirit and the unimaginable power and possibility of the Holy Spirit.

Take an example from St. John the Dwarf, who was told of a righteous young lady who, due to difficult circumstances, began to open her home to sinful people such that her home became a place of sin. He was directed to go to this young lady to help her repent, and he asked his disciples to pray that the Holy Spirit might lead and assist him in his journey. This journey resulted in St. Paisa's profound repentance and complete restoration to Christ. The Holy Spirit is therefore a spirit of change; if we knew the true power of the Holy Spirit, we would never feel despair, sadness, arrogance or doubt.

Despite all the suffering of St. Paul, he never despaired, knowing full well that the power of the Holy Spirit will overcome and change hearts. During his stay in prison, he met a thief named Onesimus. St. Paul continually prayed for him, asking the Holy Spirit to work in his heart. Onesimus saw many beautiful traits in St. Paul and liked him very much so asked him why he was like that. The answer: the power of the Holy Spirit. Eventually, Onesimus accepted the Lord Jesus Christ, was born again through baptism and is a symbol of change through the Holy Spirit.

Reflect on the golden words of the Third Hour Prayer of the Agpeya, "O Heavenly King, the Spirit of truth, the comforter, who is everywhere and fills everybody. You are the treasure of Goodness and giver of life; we ask You to graciously come and dwell within us, purify us from iniquity, O Good one and save our souls."

The Spirit Helps Our Weakness

Despite the many miracles, teachings, sayings and the power Christ displayed throughout His ministry, the initial impact on His disciples appears to have been nil. Ten of them fled, one denied Him, and one sold Him. How sad! However, Christ told them: "It is to your advantage that I go away; for if I do not go away, the Helper will not come to you; but if I depart, I will send Him to you." (John 16:7). Christ reassured them that the Helper must come to transform their weakness and spiritual poverty. Despite the richness the Lord has given us, you and I sadly live in poverty and spiritual weakness. Let us reflect and consider the different aspects of this problem, highlighting the efficacy of the Holy Spirit in providing the solution.

Let us turn to a simple story from St. Macarius the Great's 18th homily. "If a man is very rich in this world and possesses a hidden treasure, out of that treasure and wealth that he has, he purchases whatever he desires. In like manner, the person who seeks God, finds the treasure of the Holy Spirit, the Lord Himself. That treasure shines in their heart, allowing them to fulfil all the virtues, the richness, the righteousness and the goodness that God has recommended." St. Macarius adds, "So one who has found this heavenly treasure of the Spirit will follow the commandments, unblameable and pure, without forcing and with ease. Let us, therefore, beseech God [...] to bestow on us the treasure of His Spirit [...]. In contrast, if one is spiritually poor, naked, and famished in the soul, they cannot bear the fruits of the Holy Spirit."

St. Macarius gives another example, "When a rich man decides to put on a luxurious feast, he invites many people and gives generously from his riches. In like manner, those who are truly rich in the Spirit, when they speak the word in truth, they speak from within their riches and the treasure from within their souls. Simple words come from the rich treasure of the Holy Spirit within. Hence, that person affects others, unlike the poor in spirit, who have nothing to offer."

Consider the following passage from the Book of Acts, "When the Day of Pentecost had fully come, they were all with one accord in one place. And suddenly there came a sound from heaven, as of a rushing mighty wind, and it filled the whole house where they were sitting. Then there appeared to them divided tongues, as of fire, and one sat upon each of them. And they were all filled with the Holy Spirit and began to speak with other tongues, as the Spirit gave them utterance. And there were dwelling in Jerusalem, Jews, devout men, from every nation under heaven. And when this sound occurred, the multitude came together, and were confused, because everyone heard them speak in his own language." (Acts 2:1-6). We read this passage in the most important period in the Church's history – her birth – when the Apostles are filled with the Holy Spirit.

The Holy Spirit is most essential to our lives, and with that knowledge we cannot truly confess that we believe Jesus is Lord without the Holy Spirit. St. Paul tells us, "No one can say that Jesus is Lord except by the Holy Spirit." (1 Corinthians 12:3). The Holy Spirit enables humans to lead the Christian life. The disciples knew our Lord Jesus Christ through witnessing His miracles and ministry, yet Christ counselled them that they could do nothing until they received power from above.

We fall into sin because we do not let the Holy Spirit reign over our lives, granting us His power to resist the work of the devil. Even if we desire to do the work of God, we find ourselves failing and our words ineffective because we are not rich with the Holy Spirit.

In contrast, the person filled with the Holy Spirit has companionship, fellowship, and the power of the Holy Spirit within. The simplest of words makes a difference to those listening. This key difference is the work of the Holy Spirit, which is why the disciples needed to take the direction of the Holy Spirit before achieving anything, "As they ministered to the Lord and fasted, the Holy Spirit said, 'Now separate to Me Barnabas and Saul for the work to which I have called them,'" (Acts 13:2) and "A vision appeared to Paul in the night. A man of Macedonia stood and pleaded with him, saying, "Come over to Macedonia and help us." (Acts 16:9).

Even praying is the work of the Holy Spirit. As St. Paul says, "Likewise the Spirit also helps in our weaknesses. For we do not know what we should pray for as we ought, but the Spirit Himself makes intercession for us with groanings which cannot be uttered." (Romans 8:26). It is the Holy Spirit who enables you to pray. Even though you may be tired, cold or have had a long day, when you stand to pray, you receive strength, power and spiritual fire. Our saintly forefathers were confident in the power of the Holy Spirit, but unfortunately some of us are unwilling to withdraw from His power.

> ✳
> WE FALL INTO SIN BECAUSE WE DO NOT LET THE HOLY SPIRIT REIGN OVER OUR LIVES, GRANTING US HIS POWER TO RESIST THE WORK OF THE DEVIL.

When we receive the Holy Spirit during the Sacrament of Confirmation, He becomes like a fire within us will burn more strongly when given its fuel.

If the Holy Spirit is not fuelled, we extinguish Him within us. Our teacher St. Paul tells us, "Do not quench the Spirit." (1 Thessalonians 5:19). The thing which most quenches the Spirit is sin, like throwing freezing water over a fire or a candle. It ruins everything, and the person remains cold, believing they are living, but they are in fact dead. The

Bible also uses this analogy and says, "He drinks iniquity like water!" (Job 15:16).

Love – one of the fruits of the Holy Spirit – is the ignition that lights up prayer. The Holy Spirit causes joy in our service and conversations, and He fills and settles within us. It is also good to serve, as through our service we offer the Holy Spirit to others. Consider how the Apostles were transformed after they received the Holy Spirit on the Day of Pentecost, "But this is what was spoken by the prophet Joel: 'And it shall come to pass in the last days, says God, that I will pour out of My Spirit on all flesh; your sons and your daughters shall prophesy, your young men shall see visions." (Acts 2:16-17). And also: "Now when they heard this, they were cut to the heart, and said to Peter and the rest of the apostles, 'Men and brethren, what shall we do?' Then Peter said to them, 'Repent, and let every one of you be baptized in the name of Jesus Christ for the remission of sins.'" (Acts 2:37-38).

The richness of the Holy Spirit inside St. Peter the Apostle changed others. It was not his work but the work of the Holy Spirit. The Holy Spirit prepared the hearts, the time and place, and spoke gracefully on the tongue of St. Peter. This is what our fathers the Apostles experienced: working with the power and direction of the Holy Spirit through constant prayers. Compare this incredible experience with your life today: are you experiencing this power in our lives? Are you truly filled with the Holy Spirit? Is He still fiery within us, in our service, in our churches, in our minds, in our words?

Virtue Through the Treasure of the Spirit

St. Macarius contemplated that the soul must strive and struggle to earnestly ask God to be filled with the Holy Spirit. "For this reason, we should first seek from God, from the depth of our heart, the heavenly treasure of the Spirit." In the Twelfth Hour prayer of the Agpeya we read: "Out of the depths I have cried to You, O Lord; Lord, hear my voice!" (Psalm 130:1). In faith, the Holy Spirit will grant us the true treasure of Christ such that God becomes our profit and eternal life. Only when we find this treasure, can we benefit others. Christ said, "He who loves Me, will be loved by My Father, and I will love him and manifest Myself to him." (John 14:21). Christ also said, "If anyone loves Me, he will keep My word; and My Father will love him, and

We will come to him and make Our home with him." (John 14:23). Thus the home where the Holy Spirit dwells and rests is actually the soul of those who ask sincerely.

Throughout his homilies, St. Macarius speaks of the work, ways and grace of the Spirit in our lives. When the soul is filled with the Spirit, through the work of grace, the Holy Spirit works in different ways. "Grace acts upon the person invisibly in their heart, in spiritual rest. Grace deals with the person in different ways. There are times when grace comforts those born of the Spirit, making them rejoice in inexpressible joy and gladness as if entertained at a royal banquet. Other times the person reposes peacefully in communion with the heavenly bridegroom in a divine manner."

The work of the Spirit may also lead to weeping and lamentation for the sake of the sins of others. Here we pray and make supplications for the lost sheep or those who have many tribulations and suffering. At times, grace gives humility and sincerity to the heart and rejoicing in the service of and toil for others; at other times grace gives great quietness, calmness, peace and spiritual contentment. Grace also gives wisdom, understanding and knowledge of the Spirit, which is beyond examination and is not uttered with tongue or speech.

Towards the end of this homily St. Macarius says "Let us then beseech God with faith, love and immense hope, that He may grant us the heavenly grace of the gift of the Spirit, that the Spirit Himself may govern us, and guide us and lead us all into the will of God and the efficacy of grace, to restore us in all the variety of His refreshing. The Lord has promised to bestow on all those who believe in Him and ask Him in truth, the unspeakable mysteries of the Spirit. Therefore, let us devote ourselves entirely to the Lord and hasten to obtain good things."

During the period between the Ascension of our Lord and the Holy Pentecost, the goal of the disciples was to prepare themselves to receive and be filled with the Holy Spirit, "These all continued with one accord in prayer and supplication." (Acts 1:14). Their nature changed due to their prayer before God. Each time we stand before God in prayer, the Holy Spirit changes our nature. He transforms us, allowing us to accomplish things beyond our imagination.

Frequently we wonder: how can we satisfy our spirit and be filled with the Holy Spirit? Just as a child can recognise their father and mother's voices, so too the person filled with Christ's words can recognise His voice, "For in Him we live and move and have our being." (Acts 17: 28). At times we attempt to rid ourselves of a specific sin, but we fail because we work without the Holy Spirit. Therefore, we need to:

1. Practice the means of grace: prayer, fasting, service, love and giving to the poor. When we are filled with grace, we become like fire; each time it is given fuel, it ignites more.

2. Be intentional in our life, so we do not lose the divine grace. For example, if we judge others, or make our bodies impure, we grieve the Holy Spirit, and His grace leaves us.

How can a lazy person who does not pray, be pure and filled with the Holy Spirit? It is like someone trying to switch on a light without electricity. Our electricity is our prayer standing before God, tears, Bible readings, and service.

These things are the electric current required to light the lamp of the Holy Spirit in our life. We learn a beautiful lesson from our Mother St. Mary when she says, "Behold the maidservant of the Lord! Let it be to me according to your word." (Luke 1:38) She was filled with grace. The angel said to her, "Rejoice, highly favoured one [literally 'full of grace' in Greek]." (Luke 1:28).

EACH TIME WE STAND BEFORE GOD IN PRAYER, THE HOLY SPIRIT CHANGES OUR NATURE.

The Holy Spirit is humble and works in secret and invisibly within us. The Holy Spirit is very meek and gentle, but with our pride and stubbornness, we quench the Holy Spirit. The humble person, who always says yes, is a good place for the Holy Spirit to dwell and settle in. Many holy saints worked in secret, such as St. Moses the Strong, who used to walk around his monastery in the middle of the night, filling the water jars of the other monks. St. John the Short obeyed his confession father by watering a dead stick each day for three years until it miraculously grew into a huge tree. Obedience to one's confession father, the commandments and the Holy Bible, bears fruit in the fullness of time, through the Holy Spirit.

The Holy Spirit will not work if we do not want Him to. We need to begin first; then, the Holy Spirit will continue, and grace will follow.

The Spirit Covers our Spiritual Nakedness

In Genesis 3 we read of the disobedience of our mother Eve and father Adam, "So when the woman saw that the tree was good for food, that it was pleasant to the eyes, and a tree desirable to make one wise, she took of its fruit and ate. She also gave to her husband and he ate. Then the eyes of both of them were opened, and they knew that they were naked; and they sewed fig leaves together and made themselves coverings. And they heard the sound of the Lord God walking in the garden in the cool of the day, and Adam and his wife hid themselves from the presence of the Lord God among the trees of the garden. Then the Lord God called to Adam and said to him, "Where are you?" So he said, "I heard Your voice in the garden, and I was afraid because I was naked; and I hid myself." (Genesis 3:6-10). We inherited this disobedience and also live most of our life naked: not physically, but rather in spiritual nudity. We cover ourselves with false thoughts, creating a false picture of ourselves imagining we are righteous and will gain our salvation through good works.

This is the subject of St. Macarius' 20th homily "The Spirit Bearer." St. Macarius says, "If anyone is naked from the divine heavenly clothes, which is the power of the Holy Spirit, let them weep and beseech the Lord, that they may be spiritually clothed from heaven to cover their naked soul, because the person who is not covered by the Spirit is covered with shame of vile affections." Much like when a person is naked in public, there is shame and disgrace, resulting in onlookers to turn away. Consider when our father Noah stripped naked after he became drunk, and his children turned their faces away, not wanting to look at their father's nakedness. They walked backwards to put a covering over him. In the same way, the Holy Spirit covers our nakedness from within. The best part of this homily is when St. Macarius tells us that the person "must ask earnestly; weeping, crying, pleading and begging." He repeatedly uses the words 'insistence' and 'earnestly,' but to our shame we don't reach this level. We should endeavour to 'earnestly' pray until the Lord has mercy on us and clothes us with a heavenly garment.

St. Macarius continues, "When a person sees themselves naked, they are ashamed. How great is the disgrace of nakedness concerning the body? How much more is the soul when it is naked from the divine power, not realising the absence of the Holy Spirit from within? One day, this soul will stand in great shame before our Lord Jesus Christ. The naked person covers themselves with a good outer appearance to calm the conscience before others and be satisfied." St. Macarius adds, "Let this soul ask the Lord Christ, who gives glory, to be dressed in the indescribable light, not making for itself a cloak of vain thoughts, deceiving itself of self-righteousness, or fancying that it possesses the vesture of salvation." St. Macarius asserts that sin in our life primarily prevents us from enjoying the Holy Spirit and exposes our nakedness before the Lord. Of the most crucial roles of the Holy Spirit, Christ promises the Church and believers that He would send the Comforter to convict us of sin, of righteousness and of judgement.

In the Sacrament of Confirmation, the Holy Spirit dwells within us, continuously convicts us of sin and plays an essential role in our life. The Holy Spirit does not tolerate or accept impurity or evil acts. He constantly directs us towards repentance from every weakness within us, so we might not lose the Kingdom He has prepared for us. Many fathers have talked about this renewal process. Fr Tadros Malaty said, "The Holy Spirit exposes our sins to our inner vision that we might attain continuous forgiveness." The Holy Spirit is very sensitive and never exposes our weaknesses more than we can bear, lest we fall into despair. As St. Paul tells us in Romans, "Likewise the Spirit also helps in our weaknesses. For we do not know what we should pray for as we ought, but the Spirit Himself makes intercession for us with groanings which cannot be uttered." (Romans 8:26).

The Holy Spirit's role is not only to convict of sin, but also plays a significant, positive, and joyful role in revealing God's love and kindness to humankind. Throughout our continuous struggle to repent, the Holy Spirit intercedes for us, "The Spirit also helps in our weaknesses. For we do not know what we should pray for as we ought, but the Spirit Himself makes intercession for us with groaning which cannot be uttered." (Romans 8:26)

Is it any wonder the Holy Spirit has so many titles: the Intercessor, the Paraclete, the Comforter, the Advocate? The Holy Spirit stands before God the Father and intercedes for the sake of all sinners saying, "For the sake of the Blood of Your Son, save Your creation and forgive them." We don't realise and we are not aware, but that is the work of the Holy Spirit inside us. The Holy Spirit reveals our sins and encourages us to pray, to get up, and to continue the path of repentance to gain the Kingdom and eternal life. We may unexpectedly hear a sermon, read a verse, listen to part of the Liturgy or receive a message, only to find ourselves emotionally moved and regretful. We ask, "What path am I on?" This is the work of the Holy Spirit. The Holy Spirit gives us hope for fulfilling the divine promises of God's great mercies. That is why He is called the Comforter.

THE HOLY SPIRIT'S ROLE IS NOT ONLY TO CONVICT OF SIN, BUT ALSO PLAYS A SIGNIFICANT, POSITIVE, AND JOYFUL ROLE IN REVEALING GOD'S LOVE AND KINDNESS TO HUMANKIND.

The Spirit Covers our Spiritual Nakedness

St. Macarius says, "The soul needs the divine lamp (The Holy Spirit), which lightens the dark house and shines the heart. Also, the soul requires weapons because warfare against the devil is very vicious, especially in those addicted to sin. This is the meaning of the Parable of the Woman and the Lost Coin: she lights a lamp, sweeps the house, and carefully searches until she finds the coin and rejoices. Likewise, the Holy Spirit shines its light on the soul that cannot find its thoughts, enabling the soul to realise its thoughts are covered with the dirt of sin.

From the Mysteries of the Holy Spirit

Christ is the light of the world, "He who follows Me shall not walk in darkness, but have the light of life." (John 8:12). However, we sometimes find ourselves in a state of spiritual darkness; a state of stagnation in sin, where we cannot see the light of Jesus and feel no hope. The devil causes oppression of our mind, feelings and senses, thus weakening the will. We repeatedly surrender to impurity and the lust of sin without any resistance. There seems to be no hope of leaving this sin and no defiance to overcome it. St. Macarius the Great spoke of this in his 20th homily saying, "Only the Lord Jesus, with His power, can freely heal the soul." He spoke of the woman who had a blood flow for many years and had spent all her living on doctors, to no avail. As soon as she came to Christ with true faith and touched the hem of His garment, she was cured. Likewise, every soul that has incurable wounds of sin, will be healed. But only if this soul comes to the Lord Jesus Christ and prays with true faith, will they be cured and free of all corrupt desires.

St. Macarius says, "If you have no power, hope, or solution but still have the will to cry out, the Lord will hear you and save you eternally. Had not that blind man cried out or that sick woman come to the Lord, they would not have been cured. So, unless a person comes to the Lord, of their own free will, with the assurance of faith, they will find no cure." Why do we not receive the spiritual cure and salvation? It is due to a lack of faith, division of hearts, lack of love for God, and not believing in Him in truth. St Macarius concludes his homily by saying, "Let us then believe Him, come to Him, confident that He may work the true cure speedily in us. He has promised to give the Holy Spirit to those who ask Him and open to those who knock, and those who ask for Him will find Him. He who promised cannot lie."

The Holy Spirit has many mysteries in the life of Repentance, as St. John the Baptist said, "Bear fruits worthy of repentance." (Matthew 3:8). These fruits are our human deeds, but they are, in truth, the works of the Holy Spirit within us. The Holy Spirit supports the struggling person in their war against the lusts of the body and the sins of the soul. In his first letter, the Great St. Anthony wrote about the work of the Holy Spirit, who guides the mind and heart and leads the human being in practical repentance to sanctify the body to enhance spirituality. The Holy

Spirit guides us in our fasts, prayers, sleepless nights and the sweetness of repentance, bringing us into this life's delightfulness.

The Holy Spirit is the one who directs our call, makes our struggle lighter and makes our desire for repentance sweeter in our hearts. In days gone by, it was thought that this happened through our effort, but that is not the case. It is the work of the Holy Spirit in our souls to reach perfection. The body becomes sanctified through fasting, prayer, watchfulness, and service. As we suppress our bodies, the spirit of repentance becomes our guide in these matters. The Holy Spirit is the one who inspires the soul to persevere, repent and cut off the lusts of the body. Once there is a response from the human soul, the Holy Spirit like a skilful surgeon, begins to heal the soul's wounds caused by sin.

So how does the Holy Spirit heal the soul? First, He comes to the eye and gives it rules; the eye is guided to look straight ahead only at pure things. Next, the ear that would previously be thirsty for gossip, becomes sensitive to hearing only words that glorify God. The Holy Spirit then goes to the tongue and tells it "Set a guard, O Lord, over my mouth; keep watch over the door of my lips." (Psalm 141:3). The Holy Spirit goes to the hands, which previously performed many wrong actions, making them submit and sanctified as: "The lifting up of my hands as

> SPIRIT SUPPORTS THE STRUGGLING PERSON IN THEIR WAR AGAINST THE LUSTS OF THE BODY AND THE SINS OF THE SOUL.

the evening sacrifice." (Psalm 141:2). Then the stomach, which the fathers called the "The Lady of Pains" is also impacted by the Spirit removing gluttony and indulgence so that we eat only according to the needs of the body. The Holy Spirit continues down to the legs which hastened to go to inappropriate places, instructing them to be pure and to live in sanctification according to God's will. And importantly, the thoughts of lust that move within the person's mind are also impacted. The Holy Spirit redirects these thoughts and teaches the brain to distinguish what to see, hear, and eat. In all this, the Holy Spirit works invisibly and profoundly inside us.

There are two important messages here. First, we have the will, even in our weakest moments, to cry out and say, "Have mercy on me, Son of David, fill me with Your Holy Spirit. Lord, let Your Holy Spirit work within me." Second, despite the darkness and weakness that fills us, we believe and trust in God. This darkness will not overcome the light of the Holy Spirit and the authority of the Lord Jesus. Believe that the Holy Spirit will come and purify our eyes, ears, tongue, hands and thoughts and sanctify everything in us.

The Holy Spirit Working in Us

St. Macarius in his 50th homily, begins with these thought-provoking questions:

1. Did Elijah have the power to shut the doors of heaven, or was it God in him who shut the heavens and then commanded the rain?

2. When Moses laid down the rod during the ten plagues to turn it into a serpent, or when lice and frogs covered the land of Egypt: was it Moses himself, or the Hand of God who performed all these wonders?

3. When the young David engaged in battle with the giant Goliath: was it David who hurled the stone which killed the

Philistine, or the Hand of God which threw the stone and gained the victory?

4. When Joshua, the son of Nun and the leader of the Israelites, marched around the city of Jericho seven times to destroy the city walls: was it Joshua who made this happen or was it God who commanded the walls to fall?

St. Macarius closes these questions by saying: "When you hear these things, let not your mind wander far, but since these things are a symbol and shadow of the truth, apply them to yourself. When you stretch out the hands of your mind and thoughts towards heaven and set your intention to cling and unite with the Lord, Satan will fall under your thoughts." When we lift our minds and thoughts towards heaven, with great concentration and strength through the will of God, Satan will fall under our thoughts. Just as the walls of Jericho fell by the power of God, so now, by the power of God, the cities of Satan are destroyed, and the walls of evil that fight against your mind and your enemies will also fall.

St. Macarius also says: "The power of God in the Old Testament was continually present with the righteous, without ceasing, doing visible wonders; and the divine grace dwelt in the prophets inwardly. Likewise, the Spirit worked in their souls to prophesy and speak whenever there was a need to tell the world about great events. They did not always speak, but when the Spirit in them told them to, the Divine Power was always with them. Considering the Holy Spirit was poured out with vigour on the prophets in the Old Testament, which is a shadow of the covenant of grace, how much more is He poured out in the New Testament, the covenant of the cross and the coming of Christ, where the outpouring of the Spirit and its fullness occurred!"

It is written, "I will pour out of My Spirit on all flesh." (Acts 2:17) This is what our Lord Himself intended when He tells us repeatedly, "I am with you always, even to the end of the age. Amen" (Matthew 28:20); "He who seeks finds" (Matthew 7:8); "If you then, being evil, know how to give good gifts to your children, how much more will your heavenly Father give the Holy Spirit to those who ask Him!" (Luke 11:13); "Also in power, and in the Holy Spirit and in much assurance." (1 Thessalonians 1:5). St. Macarius summarises, "These things are obtained gradually, and they require time, effort, patience and much love and longing for the Lord." If you are fighting lusts, sin, or the devil's deceit and have not yet recognised the strengthening help of the Holy Spirit, then you are walking without knowing the provisions of grace and deep peace of God.

At the conclusion of each liturgy the priest says, "The love of God the Father, the grace of the Only Begotten Son and the communion and the gift of the Holy Spirit be with you all. Amen" These words originate from 2 Corinthians 13:14, "The grace of the Lord Jesus Christ, and the love of God, and the communion of the Holy Spirit be with you all. Amen" So God the Father gives love, the Son gives blessings, but the Holy Spirit gives communion because there is always an immense communion between the Holy Spirit and us. This communion with the Holy Spirit does not trap us as we remain free to accept or refuse the relationship. This is the difference between a sinner and a righteous person; a righteous person accepts the communion of the Holy Spirit and even pursues and develops it, unlike the sinner.

Filled with the Holy Spirit

One of Pope Shenouda's beautiful contemplations is, "We must revise and check over all our work and ensure that God's Spirit is sharing with us." In our prayers we ask the Holy Spirit, "God, I want to work with You as You want to work with me. Please do not separate Yourself from me and give me the power to reject any work that does not meet Your desire." What is the benefit of the Holy Spirit in any work? What will I benefit from being the temple of the Holy Spirit? Even as sinners, we must ask the Holy Spirit to help us to repent. If we decide to repent, which is a beautiful thing, we cannot do it without the help of the Holy Spirit, as it says: "Restore me, and I will return, for You are the Lord my God." (Jeremiah 31:18)

As Pope Shenouda used to encourage, we should refer to Psalm 51 as an example of repentance: "Purge me with hyssop, and I shall be clean; wash me, and I shall be whiter than snow." King David did not say, 'I will repent, or I will purify myself,' but rather 'wash me, purify me.' The Holy Spirit must participate and be the main driving power to repent, as it is impossible for us to repent alone. We are like the paralysed man, sick for 38 years without anyone to help him into the water. Or like St Peter needing to hold the hand of Christ otherwise we will drown into the sea. Our path to repentance is Him. Your Holy Spirit must reprimand me, make me feel repentant and guide me back to the spiritual path. The work of the Holy Spirit is powerful and effective.

The weakness in our spiritual life is that we depend on ourselves and not on the Holy Spirit. "Trust in the Lord with all your heart, and lean not on your own understanding." (Proverbs 3:5). Similarly, our Church service will not succeed without the Spirit of God working in it. These services are not merely activities or the work of human hands. The service of the Church will only be adequately accomplished when we participate with the Holy Spirit, "Unless the Lord builds the house, they labour in vain who build it." (Psalm 127:1) This is precisely what we saw happening in the early Apostolic Church. Even the deacons and those who served the tables, needed to be filled with the Holy Spirit.

"WE MUST REVISE AND CHECK OVER ALL OUR WORK AND ENSURE THAT GOD'S SPIRIT IS SHARING WITH US."

We need to prepare our hearts and fight the body's lusts in order to be ready to be filled with the Holy Spirit. "Walk in the Spirit, and you shall not fulfill the lust of the flesh." (Galatians 5:16). Zacharias, Elizabeth and their son John were filled with the Holy Spirit. On the Day of Pentecost, the disciples were filled with the power of the Holy Spirit when they were joined in one accord in prayer; the room was shaken, and they were all filled with the Holy Spirit. St. Peter and St. Stephen were filled with the Holy Spirit as they stood and preached their famous words. Likewise, Saul of Tarsus was filled with the Spirit, "That you may receive your sight and be filled with the Holy Spirit." (Acts 9:17) John the Beloved said, "I was in the Spirit." (Revelation 1:10).

Forcing Ourselves to Heed the Spirit Within

The strongest homily of St. Macarius is homily 19, "Christ's Commandments and the Filling of the Holy Spirit," which begins as follows: "The Christian who desires to progress and grow, ought to force themselves to do all that is good, in order to be free of indwelling sin and to be filled with the Holy Spirit."

The phrase 'force themselves' is very strong; does the Holy Spirit give, or must we force ourselves to take? St. Macarius responds with the following essential principles:

Filled with the Holy Spirit

1. If one desires to come to the Lord, be worthy of eternal life and be filled with the Holy Spirit, they must begin with:

I. Steadfast faith

II. Total submission to His commandments

III. Complete abandonment of the world

IV. Perseverance in prayer

V. Anticipation with faith for the help of the Lord.

2. We must force ourselves to do what is right and good to fulfill God's commandments. How? Since sin dwells inside us, it resists and prevents good work. Therefore, we must force ourselves to be lifted higher against the sinful inclination of our carnal hearts.

3. We must also force ourselves to be humble towards others and consider ourselves less than others. Not expecting honour, praise or glory, but rather desiring to please the Lord alone with a meek heart. "Take My yoke upon you and learn from Me, for I am gentle and lowly in heart, and you will find rest for your souls." (Matthew 11:29). Furthermore, let us accustom ourselves to being merciful, kind, compassionate and good, "Therefore be merciful, just as your Father also is merciful." (Luke 6:36) Let us always remember the humility, conduct, meekness, and life of the Lord as a permanent example before our eyes.

Persist and do not neglect your prayer. Many can admit they prefer to watch Netflix or a movie rather than pray. But instead pray before doing anything else; pleading to the Lord with faith and trust, so He may come and dwell

Forcing Ourselves to Heed the Spirit Within

in you and you become perfect in the Holy Spirit. If you wonder what the signs of are being in communion with the Holy Spirit, here are a few pointers:

1. There must be a change in the heart, "I will give you a new heart and put a new spirit within you; I will take the heart of stone out of your flesh and give you a heart of flesh. I will put My Spirit within you and cause you to walk in My statutes, and you will keep My judgments and do them." (Ezekiel 36:26-27). If I feel that the Spirit of God has changed my feelings, given me a new heart and changed my life, then I have a strong communion with the Holy Spirit. The contrast is also true: if I still have my old ways and the old creation still lives in me, I have a lot of work ahead of me.

2. Be fervent in Spirit. When the Holy Spirit came upon the disciples as tongues of fire on the Day of Pentecost, they were able to turn the world upside down. Therefore when the Holy Spirit is present within us, we feel a strong movement and a fiery zeal in our heart.

3. You are an altar of God. Like a kindled censer with black coal which turns golden when the fire ignites it, being a temple of God leads to a zealous fire seeking salvation, prayer, good deeds, reading the holy Bible and serving others. The Spirit of God is a spirit of sanctification which affects our life.

Thus, let us ask ourselves: do we live the life of sanctification which the Bible speaks of, without which no one will see God? Or do we sometimes resist the Spirit and hold on to old things? If we are truly a temple of God, then we should say with David, "Holiness adorns Your house, O Lord, forever" (Psalm 93:5) and "Be holy, for I am holy." (1 Peter 1:16).

If we commune with the Holy Spirit, we will be strong. The Lord Jesus said, "You shall receive power when the Holy Spirit has come upon you; and you shall be witnesses to Me." (Acts 1:8). We will have victory over what the devil puts before us. We can be strong in the service, resist evil thoughts and have strength over our unholy desires, "Bringing every thought into captivity to the obedience of Christ." (2 Corinthians 10:5). We will be strong in influencing others. This strength is not from us, "But we have this treasure in earthen vessels that the excellence of the power may be of God and not of us." (2 Corinthians 4:7). I urge you to evaluate the work of God in your life. Is the work of God weak, stagnant in you, like a tortoise that cannot move? Or do you feel the work of God is strong, and you feel the fire of the Holy Spirit within you?

WE MUST FORCE OURSELVES TO DO WHAT IS RIGHT AND GOOD TO FULFILL GOD'S COMMANDMENTS.

Love is the most vital sign of the Holy Spirit's communion in our lives. "Because the love of God has been poured out in our hearts by the Holy Spirit who was given to us." (Romans 5:5). The critical indicator is when we love God from all our heart, mind and soul and love our neighbour as ourselves. When the Holy Spirit grants us love towards others and peace in your heart, we know we have communion with the Holy Spirit. Truly evaluate whether the Spirit of God works in you, whether love pours out of

Forcing Ourselves to Heed the Spirit Within

your heart, and whether you have communion with the Holy Spirit. Let us pray that God gives us true communion with the Holy Spirit, accompanied by all His fruits.

Be Instructed by the Spirit

In Chapter 18 of the Book of Acts, we meet a Jewish man living in Ephesus named Apollos, "Born at Alexandria, an eloquent man and mighty in the Scriptures. This man had been instructed in the way of the Lord; and being fervent in spirit, he spoke and taught accurately the things of the Lord." (Acts 18:24-25). Take note here of the most beautiful word 'instructed', which we understand to mean 'highly trained and skilled'. What are the ways and purposes of the Lord? Answering this helps us remain eager to understand more of the work of the Holy Spirit in our path to salvation.

Let us continue with St. Macarius' 19th homily: "The Lord sees our longing, diligence and how we force ourselves to remember the Lord and to compel our heart to do what is good, even if it is against our will, obliging us to be humble, meek and love with the utmost of our strength. Then, the Lord will be compassionate and deliver us from our enemies and the indwelling sin, filling us with the Holy Spirit." Our early fathers understood the requirement for a daily 'struggle' to lead a spiritual life. Consider this quote from St. Anthony to encourage us to persist: "Let this especially be the common aim of all, neither to give way having once begun, nor to faint in trouble, nor to say: We have lived in the discipline a long time: but rather as though making a daily beginning, let us increase our earnestness."

St. Macarius continues saying, "Afterwards, without force or labour or difficulty, you will do all the Commandments of the Lord in truth." He adds, "Whoever comes to the Lord must first force themself to do what is good, even if it is against the inclination of the heart, always waiting for the mercy of the Lord, with steadfast faith. One needs to enforce love when love is lacking, meekness when there is no meekness, compassion until the heart becomes tender, bearing contempt and bear it patiently when despised or reproached or oppressed, continuing in prayer when spiritual prayer is lacking, and not become angry, as it is written, "Beloved, do not avenge yourselves." (Romans 12:19). Thus when the Lord sees us striving for Him, despite an unwilling heart, He will grant us the true prayer of the Spirit, the pleasure of true love, meekness, compassion and He will fill us with the fruits of the Spirit." Therefore, when we force ourselves to love, to be meek and to endure, the Lord looks upon our humility and honesty and says, "You have been faithful over a few things, I will make you ruler over many things." (Matthew 25:23)

Be Instructed by the Spirit

Let us consider the role of the Holy Spirit and His work for our salvation:

1. The Holy Spirit awakens us and brings us back to belief in Jesus Christ. "No one can say that Jesus is Lord except by the Holy Spirit." (1 Corinthians 12:3).

2. The Holy Spirit guides and assists us to believe in God through faith via baptism. Jesus talked about this in His meeting with Nicodemus, "Most assuredly, I say to you, unless one is born of water and the Spirit, he cannot enter the kingdom of God." (John 3:5). The heavenly birth is through baptism alone; we are adopted to become sons of our Heavenly Father, "but you received the Spirit of adoption by whom we cry out, 'Abba, Father.' The Spirit Himself bears witness with our spirit that we are children of God." (Romans 8:15-16).

3. Throughout our lives we fall into sin, but the Holy Spirit who dwells in us will open our eyes to see it, then convict us of sin in a positive way to bring us to repentance.

4. The Holy Spirit regenerates and renews us, and opens our hearts to receive His Grace, "But when the kindness and the love of God our Saviour toward man appeared, not by works of righteousness which we have done, but according to His mercy, He saved us, through the washing of regeneration and renewing of the Holy Spirit." (Titus 3:4-5). Just as St. Mary the Egyptian and St. Moses the Strong became new creations, the Holy Spirit also renews our life, heart, and mind.

5. It is in our human nature throughout our life to become confused, make mistakes or get lost. Yet the Holy Spirit will persist "He will teach you all things." (John 14:26). "For

as many as are led by the Spirit of God, these are sons of God." (Romans 8:14). We may think we are doing 'alright', but in reality are unaware of our sins. If we allow the Holy Spirit, He will warn and prevent us from falling into sin, just like He prevented the Apostles, "They were forbidden by the Holy Spirit to preach the word in Asia." (Acts 16:6).

THE HOLY SPIRIT REGENERATES AND RENEWS US, AND OPENS OUR HEARTS TO RECEIVE HIS GRACE

6. The Holy Spirit of God strengthens and empowers us to receive power from above rather than relying on our own ability to tolerate the troubles of the flesh, "Not by might, not by power, but by My Spirit, says the Lord of Hosts." (Zechariah 4:6).

7. The Holy Spirit makes us fruitful in our life, even with a simple nice word we say to others. For without the fruits of the Holy Spirit we cannot enter the Kingdom of God, "Every branch that does not bear fruit He takes away." (John 15:2). "The fruit of the Spirit is love, joy, peace, longsuffering, kindness, goodness, faithfulness, gentleness, self-control." (Galatians 5:22).

8. The Holy Spirit gives us wisdom. We experience many ups and downs in our lives, but we require wisdom to remain focussed on the Kingdom of God. This is what the oil represents in the Parable of the Five Wise and Five Foolish Virgins.

9. The Holy Spirit is the Spirit of grace, prayers and intercessions. We can't stand to pray without the guidance of the Holy Spirit; "I will pour on the house of David and on the inhabitants of Jerusalem the Spirit of grace and supplication." (Zechariah 12:10). The Holy Spirit is the one who makes us love prayer, praise, reading the Holy Bible and the saints. He satiates us.

May God open our eyes to recognise Him and understand His role in our life, so we may be like Apollos: "He had been instructed in the way of the Lord." (Acts 18:25).

Renewal in the Spirit

Since our childhood, our confession father would tell us the basic principle of spiritual life is prayer. If this was too difficult to maintain regularly, our confession father could give us a spiritual rule to adhere to, such as a specific section of prayers from the Agpeya appropriate to our age, level of spirituality, commitment and readiness to move forward. Abouna persevered with us, repeating the instructions, encouraging until we were able to stand before God in prayer and become committed, finally appreciating the importance of prayer. This is called the "enforce" principle, "The kingdom of heaven suffers violence, and the violent take it by force." (Matthew 11:12). St. Macarius the Great says in his 19th homily: "Just as you were taught to pray, so also, use the same technique for trusting in God, humility, love, meekness, sincerity, simplicity, and patience. It is of great importance to continue to force ourselves to receive these virtues."

To further progress in our spiritual life, it is essential to have a spiritual retreat in a quiet place, such as a room at home or a stroll on the beach. The aim is to quiet the spirit, calm the thoughts and meditate only on the work of God in our life. "The heavens declare the glory of God." (Psalm 19:1). St. Macarius continues: "When God sees that our heart is determined to force ourselves to have goodness, simplicity, kindness, humility and prayer, He will give us Himself in truth, and then we will be able to do all these things purely, without labour or force." The Spirit of the Lord dwells inside us and fulfils all these commandments, without effort or resistance. Sometimes divine grace comes to us while praying because God is good, kind and merciful to those who ask. The Holy Bible describes the renewal of our nature by the Spirit using three phrases: the second birth, the new creation, and the new man. Let us explore what these mean and how the Holy Spirit works in us and changes our nature:

1. The Second Birth: the Lord Jesus spoke of this with Nicodemus, "That which is born of the flesh is flesh, and that which is born of the Spirit is spirit." (John 3:6). This birth is accomplished through baptism, "Unless one is born of water and the Spirit, he cannot enter the kingdom of God;" (John 3:5) "Having been born again, not of corruptible seed but incorruptible, through the word of God which lives and abides forever." (1 Peter 1:23)

2. The New Creation: if a person is a new creation of the Holy Spirit, their attitudes completely change, as St. Paul teaches: "Therefore, if anyone is in Christ, he is a new creation; old things have passed away; behold, all things have become new." (2 Corinthians 5:17).

3. The New Man: the work of the Holy Spirit renews and gives a new nature, to change our character and makes us more inclined to goodness, holiness, righteousness, and virtue. "According to His mercy He saved us, through the washing of regeneration and renewing of the Holy Spirit." (Titus 3:5).

This is the Holy Spirit's first work – to renew our nature. On this topic St. Paul uses three juxtapositions within his epistles: the spiritual person versus the carnal, the inner person versus the outer, and the new creation versus the old.

> THEN THE SPIRIT OF THE LORD DWELLS INSIDE US AND FULFILS ALL THESE COMMANDMENTS, WITHOUT EFFORT OR RESISTANCE.

1. Spiritual versus carnal person: as St. Basil says, "The renewal which we go through in our life and our transfer from the earthly life to the heavenly life happens by the work of the Holy Spirit." Thus the carnal person does not accept God's Spirit because they are foolish and do not know Him, whereas a spiritual person has a new nature after the Holy Spirit dwells in them. The deeds of these two people are entirely different: rather than rushing after earthly desires, the spiritual person longs for heavenly rewards. Rather than pride there is humility, rather than

swearing or hatred, there is patience and blessing toward enemies. As St. Paul said, the spiritual person is entirely different from the bodily one.

2. Inner versus outer person: St. Paul says "Therefore we do not lose heart. Even though our outward man is perishing, yet the inward man is being renewed day by day." (2 Corinthians 4:16). The outer person gives attention to superficial things: appearance, image, or ego. The more the Holy Spirit works in us, the more our inner person is renewed, and the outward person perishes. Our awareness increases, our growth is no longer earthly but spiritual, and our happiest moments are when we are alone with our Lord. This is the inner person, hidden and having a strong inner relationship with God, "For indeed, the kingdom of God is within you." (Luke 17:21).

3. New versus old creation: the old person is corrupted, but the new person has the image of God who abounds in knowledge, righteousness, and holiness. St. Paul says, "That you put off, concerning your former conduct, the old man which grows corrupt according to the deceitful lusts, and be renewed in the spirit of your mind, and that you put on the new man which was created according to God, in true righteousness and holiness. (Ephesians 4:22-24). The new creation will despise earthly pleasures but because we are still in the body, we should direct all natural desires to the will of God and His glorification. The new person does not only live in this world but will live forever.

The Spirit of Truth

What is truth? In St. John's Gospel we read that Pilate entered the Praetorium during Christ's trial and curiously asked "'Are You the King of the Jews?' Jesus answered him, 'Are you speaking for yourself about this, or did others tell you this concerning Me?' Pilate answered, 'Am I a Jew? Your own nation and the chief priests have delivered You to me. What have You done?' Jesus answered, 'My kingdom is not of this world. If My kingdom were of this world, My servants would fight, so that I should not be delivered to the Jews; but now My kingdom is not from here. Pilate therefore said to Him, 'Are You a king then?' Jesus answered, 'You say rightly that I am a king. For this cause I was born, and for this cause I have come into the world, that I should bear witness to the truth. Everyone who is of the truth hears My voice.' Pilate said to Him, 'What is truth?'" (John 18:33-38). To answer this question, let us return to St. Macarius' 19th homily: "Everyone who wishes to please God in truth, and to receive from Him the heavenly grace of the Spirit, and to increase and be perfected in the Holy Spirit, ought therefore, to force themselves to follow all the commandments of God, and to subdue the heart."

One of the roles of the Holy Spirit is to guide us to the truth. The human being is weak and can easily break God's commandments. No one can do the right thing or walk on the right path without the truth, "O Lord, I know the way of man is not in himself; it is not in man who walks to direct his own steps." (Jeremiah 10:23). David the prophet said, "Teach me to do Your will, For You are my God; Your Spirit is good. Lead me in the land of uprightness." (Psalm 143:10)

Our creator has the right and the power to guide us and form us to be in His image, to be His children, and to reach His Kingdom. Knowing and following God's commandments is excellent, but He aims to unite all things in Him. St Paul says that the Holy Spirit inside us will guide us and "make you complete in every good work to do His will." (Hebrews 13:21). And just as the Lord promised His disciples, "But the Helper, the Holy Spirit, whom the Father will send in My name, He will teach you all things, and bring to your remembrance all things that I said to you," (John 14:26) and "However, when He, the Spirit of truth, has come, He will guide you into all truth." (John 13:16)

Pontius Pilate asked Jesus: "What is Truth?" The meaning of Truth in Christianity is totally different from the secular meaning. The Truth is found in Jesus Himself: "I am the way, the truth and the life. No one comes to the Father except through me." (John 14:6). Without Jesus, we cannot find any meaning in our life. And because Jesus is God, the Truth is therefore imperceptible and infinite since our human mind cannot understand the limitlessness of God. St. Philip asked Jesus, "Lord, show us the Father, and it is sufficient for us." Jesus said to him, "He who has seen Me has seen the Father." (John 14:8). Our Father grants us to know Him in the image of His only Son, who was incarnated and begotten before all ages, by the work of the Holy Spirit. If we know Jesus and live in Christ, we will know the Truth. Pontius Pilate didn't understand this because he lived in darkness, ignorance, and sin. This Truth is only known to the pure in heart, who live in purity and believe in Christ.

The problem you and I face is that we continue to break God's commandments. "Let us hear the conclusion of the whole matter: Fear God and keep His commandments, for this is man's all." (Ecclesiastes 12:13). If we want to put the meaning of Truth straightforwardly in our lives, we need to appreciate the following:

1. We belong to God, who acquired us by His blood on the cross.

2. We must strive to know Jesus and become closer to Him.

3. We are called to witness God's glory in this sinful world.

4. Live for the Truth and obey His commandments.

5. Avoid hypocrisy. If you demand Truth from others, you must also demand it from yourself.

6. Truth is a valuable treasure, but only when you live it.

The Holy Spirit is a great teacher who continuously reminds us of the Truth in Jesus. Allowed to dwell within us, the Holy Spirit enables us to practice the heavenly life and to positively expose our hearts so that we do not live in darkness. If we love Jesus, we will become more obedient to His teachings through the work of the Holy Spirit in our hearts. Those who choose darkness are unknown to God and cannot have eternal life.

The person who lives the Truth and is close to God sees the world differently through truly opened eyes. If the goal is heaven, their life will be full of thanksgiving. The early Church lived liked this to build all decisions on the Truth. In his famous sermon, St. James the Apostle says in Acts, "For it seemed good to the Holy Spirit, and to us." The Apostolic Church looked to the communion of the Truth, being led by the Holy Spirit.

> ✵
> WE ARE CALLED TO WITNESS GOD'S GLORY IN THIS SINFUL WORLD.

Outside the church, we are confronted with new different teachings. St. Cyril of Jerusalem said, "He is the great teacher of the Church; this is the Holy Spirit." And St. John says, "But you have an anointing from the Holy One, and you know all things." (1 John 2:20). Anointment from the Holy Spirit reveals the mysteries of the Lord in our hearts, opens our minds and teaches us all things, "He who has an ear, let him hear what the Spirit says to the churches." (Revelation 3:6). We must remain steadfast in our Truth and its teachings, which submits to the Holy Spirit and sheds divine light on all. As St Macarius instructs: "As we force and compel ourselves to persevere and persist in prayer, we become partakers of the Holy Spirit. Then the gift bestowed upon us will grow and thrive, resting in humility, love and meekness."

Accepting the Fiery Spirit into our Lives

The father of all monks St. Anthony the Great wrote uplifting and beneficial homilies to his children everywhere. One of these homilies – known as Sermon 8 – answers the question of how you and I can accept the fiery Spirit:

1. You have the free will to accept the Spirit and dwell in Him.

2. Offer first the labour of the body and the humility of the heart.

3. Lift your thoughts to heaven day and night, and remain persistent.

4. Ask with all your heart, for this fiery Spirit.

Filled with the Holy Spirit

Just as the Prophets Elijah and Elisha received, the Holy Spirit can be given to us also. When you have this Spirit, the mystery of heaven will be revealed to you, and greater things which cannot be written in a book will also be given to you. All your fears will be taken away and heavenly joy will overwhelm you. Such a gift should be shared, so not only ask to receive the Spirit for yourself, but for others also, Moses prayed for all the people, saying, "God, if You allow all these people to perish, blot me out of Your book also."

The Holy Spirit is a desirable companion that will attract us, sanctify us, and establish us:

1. The Holy Spirit attracts us to Christ: "But when the Helper comes, whom I shall send to you from the Father, the Spirit of truth who proceeds from the Father, He will testify of Me." (John 15:26). It is the Holy Spirit who leads the whole of humankind to the faith: "And no one can say that Jesus is Lord except by the Holy Spirit." (1 Corinthians 12:3). The main work of the Holy Spirit is to reveal to me the true nature of Christ. He honours Him and motivates me to accept the work of salvation, worship Him and draw near to Him. St. Gregory of Nyssa said, "The cause of all things, who is our Lord, shines in our hearts with the Holy Spirit, for it is impossible for the Lord Jesus to be known by truth, except by the Holy Spirit." This explains those moments when we felt the work of the fiery Spirit in our lives; that fiery worship, eagerness to pray or fast, doing prostrations, or joyfully serving with all our heart, because the Holy Spirit powerfully attracts us to do so.

2. The Holy Spirit sanctifies us: the goal of being immersed in the Spirit is to break away from everything evil and get

closer to God, to submit our life to the will of God. The Holy Spirit makes us an altar, "And no one can say that Jesus is Lord except by the Holy Spirit." (1 Corinthians 6:19). Through the Holy Chrism of the Myron in the Sacrament of Confirmation, we became a chosen vessel, dedicated for the Holy Spirit to dwell in us, "And you are Christ's, and Christ is God's." (1 Corinthians 3:23). Thus, our life belongs to Jesus, "For if we live, we live to the Lord; and if we die, we die to the Lord. Therefore, whether we live or die, we are the Lord's." (Romans 14: 8). St. Macarius the Great reflects, "The Holy Spirit that we took in the Sacrament of Myron holds the bridle of the matters in the person's life and is driven to wherever He desires. He is like two wings of the bird in the person's life." This sanctification however comes by obedience, "According to the foreknowledge of God the Father, in sanctification of the Spirit, for obedience" (1 Peter 1:2). And "Therefore, my beloved, as you have always obeyed, work out your own salvation with fear and trembling; for it is God who works in you both to will and to do for His good pleasure." (Philippians 2:12). God is working in us, but we must obey. The Holy Spirit cannot sanctify an individual without that person's will and desire to follow Jesus from all their heart.

Again, we must emphasise the Holy Spirit does not take away our freedom. We may find ourselves doing the wrong thing due to lack of obedience, due to the desires of our flesh. Without our will, we cannot get the Holy Spirit as our helper. St. Augustine says, "We do not achieve our goal without our will, but we cannot achieve our goal unless we get the Holy Spirit, the Helper." God supports us with the power of the Holy Spirit.

3. The Holy Spirit establishes us in Jesus: our Lord Jesus spoke often about this, "I am the vine, you are the branches. He who abides in Me, and I in him, bears much fruit; for without Me you can do nothing." (John 15:5). St. John also says, "Now he who keeps His commandments abides in Him, and He in him. And by this we know that He abides in us, by the Spirit whom He has given us," (1 John 3:24) and "No one has seen God at any time. If we love one another, God abides in us, and His love has been perfected in us." (1 John 4:12). The invitation to 'abide' is the key, "If anyone loves Me, he will keep My word; and My Father will love him, and We will come to him and make Our home with him." (John 14:23).

> THE HOLY SPIRIT IS A DESIRABLE COMPANION THAT WILL ATTRACT US, SANCTIFY US, AND ESTABLISH US.

In the words of St. Athanasius, "When the Holy Spirit has been given to us, He raises God in us," and if God is in us, the Son is in us, and we may joyfully walk with an upright heart.

The Holy Spirit Renews our Image to be that of Christ's

In his 30th homily "Born of the Holy Spirit," St. Macarius the Great gives us some valuable exercises. "For an artist to draw a portrait of a king's face, the king must keep his face attending to the painter so that he may draw him accurately. However, once the king turns his face away from the artist, it becomes difficult for the artist to draw the king's image because the face of the king is not gazing at the artist. In like manner, Christ the good artist, for those who believe in Him and have their gaze continually on Him, portrays a divine image for us, in the image of God and bestows on us a gorgeous, heavenly grace. Hence, to have the image of Christ, we must continuously gaze our eyes upon Him, living in Christ, believing Him, loving Him, and following Him with all our hearts. We must reject all else for Christ to paint His divine image on us and graft it into our souls, thus, wearing Christ inside us to receive eternal life and rest. Also, just as a gold coin, if it does not have the image of the king imprinted on it, it is rejected in the marketplace and is not stored in the king's treasuries and hence, discarded. Likewise, the soul that does not have the image of the divine Spirit imprinted on it, will be unfit for the treasuries and discarded."

St. Macarius also discusses the Parable of the Servants and the Invitation to the Wedding as recounted in Matthew 22. He says, "The person who is invited and is not wearing the wedding garment is cast out into the darkness since they are not wearing the heavenly image." This is the mark and the sign of the Lord imprinted upon our souls, the mark of the eternal, heavenly world. The Divine Spirit is the life of the soul; without it, the soul is dead and has no life in the eternal heavenly world. Therefore, those who seek the Lord should ask and plead to receive the Divine Spirit here on earth, for that Spirit is the life of the soul. When a bird flies high, it is neither worried about nor afraid of hunters or predators since its height keeps it safe from them. Likewise, when the soul attains the wings of the Spirit and flies to heavenly heights, it will be above all the enemies below.

Let us consider how the Holy Spirit renews our image to resemble Christ:

1. The Holy Spirit announces the presence of Jesus in us: after his resurrection Jesus promised His disciples,

The Holy Spirit Renews our Image to be that of Christ's

"Lo, I am with you always, even to the end of the age." (Matthew 28:20). But how exactly? We cannot experience the presence of Jesus without the Holy Spirit. He is the one who repeats the voice of God inside us. The Saints confirmed this through their own experiences. St. John Chrysostom, the Golden Mouth who has the Spirit dwelling in him, said the Holy Spirit could not be present without Jesus being present because if one of the Divine Hypostases is present, the Holy Trinity is also present. Also St. Athanasius says, "The Holy Spirit has never been separated from The Word. For verification, when the Lord said I will come with the Father, the Spirit will come with them too, dwell inside us, not for any reason but for the Son to dwell in us."

2. The Holy Spirit changes our image to God's image: as St. Macarius said in homily 30, "'But we all, with unveiled face, beholding as in a mirror the glory of the Lord, are being transformed into the same image from glory to glory, just as by the Spirit of the Lord.' (2 Corinthians 3:18) The Holy Spirit is the one who completes this change in us by promoting a steady growth, as long as we obey our Lord and submit to Him through His commandments, His words in the Scriptures and our life with Him." The Holy Spirit wants to deeply imprint Jesus' image on the hearts of people who accept Him. St. Cyril of Alexandria also spoke about this saying, "As God Created man in His own image and likeness, so all the generations which follow will be changed to be like Him, through the gift of the Holy Spirit. Without a doubt, it is the Holy Spirit who puts the stamp of the image of the Saviour on the hearts of those who accept Him."

3. The Holy Spirit proclaims the love of God in us: Origen the scholar said, "The Holy Spirit is the Spirit of the Father and the Spirit of the Son; we are in need for Him to dwell inside us, to proclaim to us that God is love, not through theological words or thoughts or philosophy, but through the presence of the true, divine love inside us. The spirit of truth who proceeds from the Father, who wanders, searching for the souls worthy of accepting this great love, which is God."

4. The Holy Spirit gives us strength: when Christ was among the people, He was the source of their strength and power. However, after His ascension, He sent His strength and power to His disciples through the Holy Spirit. "But you shall receive power when the Holy Spirit has come upon you; and you shall be witnesses." (Acts 1:8). They could do nothing in their ministry – preaching or spreading the word – without the Holy Spirit. The Holy Spirit completes any weakness or imperfections within us. This is demonstrated in the Book of Acts when St. Peter speaks with mighty power from God in his sermon. The Holy Spirit turned St. Paul's life around and helped the disciples begin their mission of spreading the Faith to the Church. Compare how frightened and fearful the disciples were before receiving the Holy Spirit in the upper room, to the strength and power with which they preached after they received the Holy Spirit. "But Elymas the sorcerer (for so his name is translated) withstood them, seeking to turn the proconsul away from the faith. Then Saul, who also is called Paul, filled with the Holy Spirit, looked intently at him and said, "O full of all deceit and all fraud, you son of the devil, you enemy of all righteousness, will you not cease perverting the straight ways of the Lord? And now,

indeed, the hand of the Lord is upon you, and you shall be blind, not seeing the sun for a time." (Acts 13:8-11). Also, when St. Paul stood before Felix the Governor, we see how the governor was terrified; "My speech and my preaching were not with persuasive words of human wisdom, but in demonstration of the Spirit and of power." (1 Corinthians 2:4).

St. Basil the Great teaches us that renewal by the Holy Spirit is a guarantee for those who believe. "The Holy Spirit gives us the power of renewal. As for how this happens, that is something beyond rational logic. It is a mystery, and the fruits of this renewal are evident in the salvation of our souls." He says, "The renewal is the transition and change from our earthly life that we live, to the heavenly, spiritual life, by the work of the Holy Spirit. By Him, we return to paradise and are lifted to the kingdom of heaven. This is the adoptive call; the evidence is that we call God 'our Father.' With the Holy Spirit we have become partakers of Christ and are called children of light. We become partakers in the everlasting glory and the fullness of the blessing."

> TO HAVE THE IMAGE OF CHRIST, WE MUST CONTINUOUSLY GAZE OUR EYES UPON HIM

It is no surprise that we are pressed by sin or trials in our life daily, but we must realise the only way to overcome these pressures and be renewed is through the mighty power of the Holy Spirit who dwells in us. He gives us the authority to conquer the world, "to execute vengeance on the nations and punishments on the peoples; to bind their kings with chains... this honour have all His saints." (Psalm 149).

The Holy Spirit is Our Comforter and Advocate

In the Old Testament, the purpose of the prophecies was to point to the Spirit and the Incarnation of Christ. The people were comforted by the anticipated arrival of the Messiah. However, after Christ's death, resurrection and ascension into heaven, there was a need for another comforter. "And I will pray the Father, and He will give you another Helper, that He may abide with you forever— the Spirit of truth, whom the world cannot receive, because it neither sees Him nor knows Him; but you know Him, for He dwells with you and will be in you." (John 14:16-17). That is why we say in the third hour prayers of the Agpeya, "O' heavenly King, the Spirit of truth, the comforter."

The Greek word for "Comfort" is "Parakletos", which also means "Advocate." St. Cyril of Jerusalem said, "He is called the comforter because He comforts us and encourages us, assists us in our weakness. Often, we are despised and unjustly humiliated for the sake of Christ, with problems around us from everywhere, but the Holy Spirit quietly whispers, 'Wait for the Lord, lift your eyes to the Lord, He will come at the right time.' This is the voice of the Holy Spirit within us, as the Comforter." When you or I attempt to comfort others in times of crisis, we can often be burdensome or not successful in easing their pain. On the other hand, although we do not know how He comforts those who have lost loved ones, He truly comforts them. He is a true Comforter.

This is the work of the Holy Spirit in our lives: He will teach us everything, He will tell us things to come, He will take from what is in Christ and give to us. He will remind us of what Jesus has said, and He will rest within us, allowing all believers to do great things. So how exactly does the Holy Spirit comfort us?

1. Gives us peace: when the Holy Spirit came upon the Church on the day of Pentecost, He started calming the fearful and troubled hearts of those gathered in the upper room. "Then the churches throughout all Judea, Galilee, and Samaria had peace and were edified. And walking in the fear of the Lord and in the comfort of the Holy Spirit, they were multiplied." (Acts 9:31).

2. Gives us Hope: in Romans, St. Paul says, "Now may the God of hope fill you with all joy and peace in believing, that you may abound in hope by the power of the Holy Spirit." (Romans 15:13).

3. Gives us Courage: God promises all His people encouragement throughout all generations and centuries. Even in the Old Testament, "'According to the word that I covenanted with you when you came out of Egypt, so My Spirit remains among you; do not fear!'" (Haggai 2:5).

4. Gives us Reassurance and Calmness: the voice of the Holy Spirit always reassures and calms us and gives us hope when we despair.

St. Gregory the Great said, "The word Paraclete in Latin is Lawyer, because He stands before the throne of God, before the justice of the Heavenly Father, to account for sinful sinners. He stands and pleads with zeal as St. Paul said, "The Spirit Himself makes intercession for us with groanings which cannot be uttered." (Romans 8:26).

The Holy Spirit supports us in our struggle against the devil's cunning fight; through our weak mind, behaviour, and senses we may fall into sin. But we should not forget we have a companion – the Comforter the Paraclete – who is the ultimate Advocate and Lawyer, who stands for us and defends us so long as we hear His whispers and His voice within our hearts. In our daily

THE HOLY SPIRIT SUPPORTS US IN OUR STRUGGLE AGAINST THE DEVIL'S CUNNING FIGHT;

struggle in prayer and all the means of grace, we come closer to God by the help of the Holy Spirit.

The Immense Gifts of the Spirit in our Lives The

Let us examine St. Macarius' 11th Homily entitled, "Lord Jesus, enter deeply in our heart and lift us up." St. Macarius meditates and says, "When Jesus performed this glorious work by going down to hell to deliver all the souls from hell and darkness, we imagine that these things are historical and removed from us, but the Lord does all these works in our soul." St. Macarius explains how the devil imprisons the soul in much detail and very graphically. The explanations give us insight into the greatness of saints like St. Macarius, to whom God has revealed these things.

Filled with the Holy Spirit

St. Macarius says, "We have the ability to receive the devil inside us and accept him in our life. Death will hold the mind of the person. Just like it is inside tombs, sometimes your heart is a grave and burial for the ruler of demons and his soldiers to enter the heart, thoughts and minds and make a path and access there. In front of others, the person is living, talking, eating and drinking, but before God, it is a dead person, living in ignorance, a stranger, away from God." He gives another example: "If a person binds their hands and legs with chains and is thrown into the sea, they are unable to swim and are surrounded by terrifying sea creatures. How can anyone go down to this person in the sea unless they are a strong and clever swimmer who is able to control these sea creatures? Or who can go down into this dark chamber, in the depths of hell and death, to save this person, except that expert Workman, who created the body and the soul? There is no difficulty for God to enter death, into graves, into the depth of hell. This is His work just as He did before; He can even do it if everything is blocked."

St. Macarius continues this contemplation, "Sometimes the devil talks to our heart saying, 'See how many evils you did, how many foolish things you did. You are full of sin, which can't be saved?'" Here the devil attempts to make us fall into despair. This is dangerous and can affect our spiritual life because we feel that even repentance is unacceptable. The devil continues to speak to us, convincing us of this. But St. Macarius reassures

LORD JESUS, ENTER DEEPLY IN OUR HEART AND LIFT US UP.

us, "Remember my beloved, that the Lord came down and was incarnated to save the sinners, to raise the dead and to revive the souls that perished and to give light to those in darkness. In truth, He came and called us to be adopted children. When this voice comes to us, remember God's words, "I have no pleasure in the death of the wicked, but that the wicked turn from his way and live." (Ezekiel 33:11)." He concludes by saying, "Let us remain in poverty, alienated and enduring suffering, pleading and praying, earnestly knocking on the Lord's door, for the Lord is near to us, even more than the soul is to the body. Therefore, He comes and opens the closed doors of our hearts and pours His heavenly riches and blessings on us. He is good, loving, kind and merciful. His promises are true without lies if we continue to seek Him to the end, continuously calling His Holy Spirit."

The Holy Spirit has many strategies to rescue us from the depths of sin:

1. The Holy Spirit convicts us when we sin: St. Enemos says, "If God did not love the soul, He would not have been jealous of her and would not have pursued her for the love of others. Like a groom who pursues his bride for her love." If you or I become upset with someone, we could block or delete their number... but not so with God! His love for us is zealous, and He sends His Holy Spirit to urge and push us towards repentance. The love of God never perishes; He is so patient with us until we return to Him. As an exercise, look back on your own life and count the times God was patient with you.

2. The Holy Spirit pierces our hearts: "Today, if you will hear His voice, Do not harden your hearts." (Hebrews

3:15). Consider those who entered the Christian faith on the day of Pentecost, "When they heard this, they were cut to the heart," (Acts 2:37). The Holy Spirit moderates our insight to see within ourselves and atone for our sins, bit by bit to reveal the sins within us gradually so we don't fall into despair or have low self-esteem. Once we repent, he reveals the next sin, and so on. St. Macarius says, "What does a person do to discover sin, know it, distinguish it, and cast it far away? Here we need the Divine Lamp, the Holy Spirit, who enlightens and renews the dark place."

3. The Holy Spirit sanctifies and purifies us: one of the most used words for holiness in the New Testament is "agios" [holy] with all its derivatives. It is said over 230 times. What is the source of holiness? It is God. When we are separated from Him, our holiness is also far. As we draw closer to Him, through all the means of grace, Holy Communion, Bible reading, prayer, repentance, confession, and service, we return to His holiness. "And you shall be holy to Me, for I the LORD am holy." (Leviticus 20:26). Origen says, "The power of sanctification is the grace of God, the grace of the Holy Spirit which sanctifies us."

4. The Holy Spirit adopts us: He is the one who gives us a sense of sonship to say 'Our Father', "For as many as are led by the Spirit of God, these are sons of God. For you did not receive the spirit of bondage again to fear, but you received the Spirit of adoption by whom we cry out, 'Abba, Father.' The Spirit Himself bears witness with our spirit that we are children of God." (Romans 8:14).

5. The Holy Spirit supports us: from the time of confirmation until we leave this earth, we have the Holy Spirit within us. The devil continues to fight us throughout our life;

however, the Holy Spirit stands beside us, protects us, encourages us and praises us. St. Cyril of Jerusalem says, "Do not fear Satan, because inside us we carry an extreme power; the Holy Spirit who dwells inside us and protects us like a soldier who stands beside us day and night."

6. The Holy Spirit gives us spiritual growth: this may be achieved via a combined effort between us and the Holy Spirit. St. Anthony says, "Just like when trees and plants do not survive without water, likewise, the soul cannot grow and be uplifted if it does not accept the heavenly joy, which is the Holy Spirit."

7. The Holy Spirit gives us true humility: all our saintly fathers and mothers that we read about were powerful and strong, filled with the fruits of the Holy Spirit. They attained this because of their humility which we too can aim for.

The Holy Spirit teaches us pure, true prayers acceptable before God. We receive knowledge, enlightenment, spiritual wisdom and by far the most desirable gift: eternal life.

Bearing the Fruits of the Holy Spirit - Love

The Scriptures reveal many teachings about bearing fruits, even before Christ's coming. St. John the Baptist says, "Bear fruits worthy of repentance." (Matthew 3:8). In the Gospel of St. Matthew, Jesus says, "Either make the tree good and its fruit good, or else make the tree bad and its fruit bad; for a tree is known by its fruit," (Matthew 12:33) and "A good man out of the good treasure of his heart brings forth good things." (Matthew 12:35). In the Gospel of St. John, Jesus tells us of the relationship between the fruit, the branches and the vine, "I am the true vine and my Father is the vinedresser. Every branch in Me that does not bear fruit, He takes away; and every branch that bears fruit He prunes, that it may bear more fruit." (John 15:2). Also, "For without Me you can do nothing... By this My Father is glorified, that you bear much fruit; so you will be My disciples." (John 15:5-8). The obvious theme from Christ is the fruits in our life.

Our saintly fathers also speak about bearing fruits. St. Cyril of Jerusalem says, "When a soul lives in sin and then enters the stage of repentance, this soul becomes worthy of the Holy Spirit to bear much fruit. Although the Holy Spirit is one, the virtues and the fruits that work in the soul are many." St. Augustine says, "When Jesus said, 'Make the tree and its fruits good,' He did not mean this to be just advice or a suggestion, but rather a commandment that must be obeyed. It is a command and warning that the person must change their ways and works to be worthy of being filled with the Holy Spirit. Only by doing this will they produce fruits." St. Macarius the Great says, "The naked soul that has no communion with the Holy Spirit is like the poor person who cannot offer anything, not even fruits produced in life. But the soul who enters into a strong relationship with the Holy Spirit, the soul who finds the Lord, the soul who finds the treasure, the soul who asks for the Spirit with faith, trust and patience, will bring forth many fruits." The word 'patience' is significant; it is a long spiritual path for the soul to produce fruit which cannot be done without patience and steadfastness in God.

In His Sermon on the Mount, Christ taught us about love through the Beatitudes. Before He left, He commanded the Church concerning love in the Gospel of St. John, the Paraclete Chapters. If we want to preach the Gospel in His name, and to be the salt of the earth and a light to shine in the darkness in this world, we need to love one another. Love is His greatest commandment: "'Teacher, which is the great commandment in the law?' Jesus said to him, 'You shall love the Lord your God with all your heart, with all your soul, and with all your mind.' This is the first and great commandment. And the second is like it: 'You shall love your neighbour as yourself.' On these two commandments hang all the Law and the Prophets" (Matthew 22:36-39).

St. Paul frequently spoke of the fruits of the Holy Spirit. "But the fruit of the Spirit is love…" (Galatians 5:22). We can't forget the great love symphony that St. Paul spoke of in 1 Corinthians 13 just after he finished outlining the gifts of the Holy Spirit, "And yet I show you a more excellent way." (1 Corinthians 12:31). St. Paul tells us that love is the greatest symphony known to humankind and the greatest of all virtues. It is more significant than speaking in tongues, prophecy, and even greater than faith. Love is the only common language the universe agrees on, which we cannot live without. "God is love." (1 John 1:8).

Love is like a fountain; when it is open, it yields all the other fruits.

How can we encourage the Spirit to bear love within us?

1. Prayer is love: sit at the feet of Jesus and be filled by Him.

2. Service is love: we give ourselves to others for the sake of Jesus.

3. Repentance is love: we please God and accept the good part.

Filled with the Holy Spirit

4. Reading the Bible is love: we prefer to sit at Jesus' feet and hear His words.

Sadly, love can fade when we are far from God and busy with earthly matters. In the Book of Revelation, St. John records the words of Christ to the angel of the Church of Ephesus, "Nevertheless I have this against you that you have left your first love. Remember therefore from where you have fallen, repent and do the first works, or else I will come to you quickly and remove your lampstand from its place." (Revelation 2:4-5). Our Lord has much patience and long suffering, but when we leave our first love because we become too busy with other things, He reminds us to return to Him and repent. God always desires us to be in a strong relationship with Him, but often we favour everything other than Jesus. In contrast, our saintly mothers and fathers never let anything in the world separate them from their Lord Jesus. This was because they tasted the Lord; they felt Him and the great love that comes from Him. St. Anthony sold all his possessions to follow Jesus and live in a cave. St. Bishoy tied his hair with a string to the roof in order to stay awake and pray all night because of his great love for the Lord Jesus. St. Anna Simone, the humble queen; the more she was humiliated, the more she loved the Lord. She rejoiced in all the insults because they drew her into a more profound love for Christ.

IF WE WANT TO PREACH THE GOSPEL IN HIS NAME, AND TO BE THE SALT OF THE EARTH AND A LIGHT TO SHINE IN THE DARKNESS IN THIS WORLD, WE NEED TO LOVE ONE ANOTHER.

Divine love is different from earthly love. The love of God is like a mighty fire, touching everyone around us; it fills the heart and then overflows onto others. The Holy Spirit purifies our hearts from earthly desires, envy and greed. Lukewarmness in our spiritual life occurs when we lose love for Christ, which means the Holy Spirit cannot work in us. St. Paul says, "Because the love of God has been poured out in our hearts by the Holy Spirit who was given to us." (Romans 5:5). Therefore, when we are filled and have communion with the Holy Spirit, love will be poured on us and those around us also. For the Holy Spirit to pour love on us, we must first cleanse our heart from other distractions: desires, greed, envy and evil works.

Take a moment to reflect honestly on the following:

1. Where has my first love gone?

2. Is my love now as pure as it once was?

3. Do I grow in love, or does most of my love come from others?

4. Do I have more love or more hatred in my relationship with others?

Anything we do in love has a different and unique taste. "I found the one I love. I held him and would not let him go." (Song of Songs 3:4). The sign that the Holy Spirit is within us is the love that reigns in our hearts. The sign of success of the Holy Spirit is the flood of love that pours freely onto others.

Bearing the Fruits of the Holy Spirit-Joy

And In his 40th homily St. Macarius the Great introduces the concept of a 'Spiritual Chain'. "All virtues and external practices are connected like a chain; hence, prayers are linked with love, love brings joy, joy is connected to meekness, meekness with humility, humility helps you to serve with hope, hope with faith, faith with obedience to the guidance of the Holy Spirit and obedience is linked to simplicity. As the virtues have a linked chain, so also disgrace has a linked chain. Hate, linked with resentment and anger, anger with pride, pride with lack of faith, hardens the heart, leading to neglect, laziness, boredom, then loss of patience, which leads to the love of lusts." We often do not realise the deep wisdom of our Fathers to share such spiritual insights beyond what we see, given to them because they lived in prayer, calmness and meditation.

St. Macarius continues, "Every good work, virtue, power and benefit in our life is due to the perseverance of prayer." You and I have a handy list of excuses to avoid praying; we expertly convince ourselves that we are too busy, or it's too hard, or too much effort. To this St. Macarius says, "Prayer generates within us communion with the Holy Spirit and generates in us a spiritual energy, a positive energy, and gradually our mind becomes linked and attached to God." He creates indescribable love in us, and for this reason, he tells us to force ourselves, to push ourselves each day to pray. This push ignites our divine love and gives us a strong desire to grow towards God and attain the perfect sanctification of our spirit.

The second fruit of the Holy Spirit is joy. Christianity always invites us to be joyful and not wallow in sorrow and sadness. This joy does not come from our own achievement, but rather from the Holy Spirit inside us, just as the rays that proceed from the sun. Numerous verses in the Bible speak of joy; "For the Kingdom of God is not eating and drinking, but righteousness and peace and joy in the Holy Spirit." (Romans 14:17). "And the disciples were filled with joy and with the Holy Spirit." (Acts 13:52). Even St. Paul during his tribulations, "As sorrowful, yet always rejoicing," (2 Corinthians 6:10), and St. James, "My brethren, count it all joy when you fall into various trials." (James 1:2). Joy is the characteristic of a genuine Christian.

Bearing the Fruits of the Holy Spirit-Joy

Look around you now, at the coffee shop or in your office: it is hard to find genuinely joyful people. A Google search to find a few Bible verses is easy but finding them within our hearts and living by them is challenging. Our Lord Jesus Christ is available to assist us if we ask Him to grant the words that we read to become living words, authentic and genuine in our daily life.

St. Paul's epistle to the Philippians is known as the epistle of Joy. One might assume this was because he was living comfortably, finally rid of his haters and swimming in praise. Quite the opposite in fact, he was trapped in prison! St. Paul did not blame God – as we often do – and it was in fact his preaching about God which was the reason for his predicament. He could have become resentful about his circumstances, angry, bitter or depressed, abandoning his service. But instead, he wrote the most beautiful epistle of Joy in the Bible. If we analyse how he managed this in such trying circumstances, then you and I can strive to replicate this in our own life to receive such joy:

1. Prayer and praise: these are the first sources of joy in his life which he shared with those around him. "But at midnight Paul and Silas were praying and singing hymns to God, and the prisoners were listening to them." (Acts 16:25). In order to have joy, we need to have communion with God and be a prayerful person. No one can deny that we may gain much pleasure from this world, but this is foolish as it is not real joy. True joy for a Christian requires daily standing in prayer which as St. Macarius teaches us, awakens the Holy Spirit.

2. Have a goal: when St. Paul was chained to the walls in prison, he did not mind as it did not hinder his goal to

preach and build the Kingdom of Heaven. Other prisoners and even the guards listened to his message and became believers. This is because he had a goal that gave meaning to his life. But what is our goal nowadays? One goal – and probably the best – is to give glory to God. If we are confined to earthly goals, our life will resemble the stock market: going up and down with no certainty. However, if our goal is spiritual, we have inner joy through closeness with prayer. St. Paul rightly believed that people's opinion of him was the least of his worries. What God saw in Him was more important, giving him freedom. Likewise you and I, the less we care about the opinion and approval of others, the more we will feel lighter and gain freedom of joy in our mind, thoughts, and movement.

> ❋
> EVERY GOOD WORK, VIRTUE, POWER AND BENEFIT IN OUR LIFE IS DUE TO THE PERSEVERANCE OF PRAYER

Another weight we must unburden ourselves from to reach the heights of joy is our ego. The solution is giving. Sharing our time, love, money, emotions and kindness. The more we share, the more joy will return to us allowing us to be truly satisfied and content. St. Paul's epistle to the Philippians contains one of the most famous verses: "I can do all things through Jesus Christ who strengthens me" (Philippians 4:13).

Many people with abundant material possessions remain unhappy, sad or depressed; they covet what does not belong to them and this robs them of happiness and joy.

Again, the imprisoned St Paul celebrates: "In all things I have learned both to be full and to be hungry, both to abound and to suffer need." (Philippians 4:12). In contrast, reducing worldly things allows us to turn our eyes to heaven and rejoice because God fills us with abundant good things from within. For this reason, the contented person is always joyful. With practice and commitment, the Holy Spirit will give us true joy, peace and reconciliation with ourselves and others.

Bearing the Fruits of the Holy Spirit- Peace

Most of the characters we read about in the Bible have a common virtue: patience. Consider how long our father Abraham waited for the promise of his offspring Isaac. Moses fled from Egypt to Midian and waited while the Lord prepared him. Joseph waited patiently for over a decade to see God's plan for his life. David waited as a simple shepherd for almost 20 years while God prepared him to be the king of Israel. Patience is an essential virtue for growth in our spiritual life. Today we have been programmed to expect great speed and efficiency and therefore miss out on the opportunity for peace. Peace is the silence of the inner life and the third fruit of the Holy Spirit.

To understand what peace truly is, consider its opposite: being irritated and restless, needing to achieve more and more to feel temporarily happy. Such a person thinks 'I would pay any amount of money to have some peace and quiet.' In his 31st homily "Waiting for the Lord inside," St. Macarius the Great says, "If we want to please God in every service we offer Him, strive to please Him while waiting for Him within ourselves since He is in our heart. Examine your thoughts and compel your will and intentions towards Him. "The Lord will come and make our home with Him." (John 14:23). Gather your minds, thoughts and desires to seek Him without laziness or carelessness. Then the Lord, when He sees your diligence in seeking Him, manifests Himself, appears to you, and gives us great support and victory. Hence, when our Lord looks at us and sees how long we have waited for Him, with continuous hope, He will teach us true prayer and true love. He will be inside us, and we will feel His presence like a precious pearl, and then we will feel the Kingdom of Heaven within us."

Peace is a gift from God, and the God of peace gives us peace; "For unto us a child is born, and His name will be called Wonderful, Counsellor, Mighty God, Everlasting Father, Prince of Peace." (Isaiah 9:6). Just before our Lord Jesus' suffering, He said to His disciples: "Peace I leave with you, My peace I give to you; not as the world gives do I give to you. Let not your heart be troubled, neither let it be afraid." (John 14:27). Similarly, the Bible reminds us continually about peace, "Live in peace and the God of love and peace will be with you." (2 Corinthians 13:11) and "Depart from evil and do good; seek peace and pursuit it." (Psalm 34:14). Simon the Elder said, "Lord, now You are letting Your servant depart in peace, according to Your word." (Luke 2:29).

Our Church continuously wishes this peace on her children. At the end of each service the priest or bishop will say to the congregation, "Go in peace, the peace of the Lord be with you all," and we reply, "And also with you." There are three constituents to peace from the Holy Spirit:

1. Peace with God: when God created man and woman, they were at peace with God and had a good relationship with Him. But peace was lost the second they committed sin. "There is no peace," says the Lord, "for the wicked." (Isaiah 48:22). Peace therefore comes to us through a life of repentance to return to God. The best gift that God gives us after we repent is the feeling of his Godly peace spreading to every corner of our being. St. Paul says, "Therefore, having been justified by faith, we have peace with God through our Lord Jesus Christ." (Romans 5:1). One who depends on themselves and does not surrender their life to God cannot have peace just as St. Augustine says, "Our hearts are restless until they rest in You."

2. Peace with people: harmony and love with others allows us to share emotions and intentions. God prefers harmony and peace amongst us rather than sacrifices and rituals. "Therefore if you bring your gift to the altar, and there remember that your brother has something against you, leave your gift there before the altar, and go your way. First be reconciled to your brother, and then come and offer your gift." (Matthew 5:23-24). Peace with every single person in our life sounds impossible since we cannot change people or the world, but it is achievable; we must accept the things we cannot change, nurture a gentle,

humble spirit and an open heart. "If it is possible, as much as depends on you, live peaceably with all men." (Romans 12:18).

The church may preclude a person from receiving Holy Communion if they have had a dispute with another person and reconciliation with this person is required to receive the sacrament of Communion. We need to bear with and forgive others, realising that whoever bears the mistakes of others is the stronger one, not the one who rages and becomes angry. As St. Paul tells us, "We then who are strong ought to bear with the scruples of the weak, and not to please ourselves." (Romans 15:1).

3. Peace with ourselves – reconciling with oneself is possible through repentance, grace and purity. Those close to God feel an inner comfort and peace, echoing the words of king David, "Yea, though I walk through the valley of the shadow of death, I will fear no evil, for You are with Me." (Psalm 23:4). Enduring tribulations, experiencing problems at work or with our relationships make it difficult to have peace. How then can we keep it in these difficult situations? Faith and trust. God's tenderness exudes peace and joy to our hearts, allowing us to pass through times of darkness if we surrender to Him. Faith gives hope, hope gives patience, patience gives peace, and peace gives joy. "So when the ship was caught, and could not head into the wind, we let her drive." (Acts 27:15)

For those of us who require a practical exercise, take the advice

RECONCILING WITH ONESELF IS POSSIBLE THROUGH REPENTANCE, GRACE AND PURITY.

of St. Athanasius the Apostolic who once said, "Anyone who is troubled or sad and sees the face of St. Anthony will gain peace." St. Anthony was a man filled with the Holy Spirit, so keep a small picture of him in your office or desk, or wherever you find it most difficult to experience this fruit of the Holy Spirit.

Bearing the Fruits of the Holy Spirit- Longsuffering

In his 4th homily, "God's patience and His great kindness," St. Macarius the Great spoke of learning patience and kindness from the Bible. "Look to Israel, where all the fathers came. God gave them promises, and from them, Christ came in the flesh, with worship services and signs of covenant. Throughout the major and minor prophets, we see how they sinned and turned away from God. However, our Lord did not leave them but rather disciplined them for a while due to the hardness of their hearts and brought them back to Him again. How often did they sin and anger the Lord while He was patient with them? When they returned to Him with all their hearts, He rejoiced and forgave them."

When Christ came, He was not accepted by the Jews, but instead they insulted Him and sentenced Him to death. But our good King has patience with us; despite every sin against Him, He waits for us to return and repent, and heaven rejoices with the return of each sinner. "Even so it is not the will of your Father who is in heaven that one of these little ones should perish." (Matthew 18:14). As we say in the Gregorian Liturgy, He did not limit His love towards humankind.

Learning from His example, longsuffering is essential for you and I when dealing with others. How many quarrels and misunderstandings could be avoided with our siblings, parents or colleagues? Longsuffering is once again gained through the Holy Spirit. It is a mighty virtue that allows the individual to bear matters with meekness and be patient in injustice, insults and annoyance from others. Christ gives us lessons in patience and longsuffering: "How often shall my brother sin against me, and I forgive him?" Jesus said to him, "Up to seventy times seven." (Matthew 18:21). There is no gain in boiling up within and getting revenge later.

In the example of the plant not bearing fruit, Jesus says, "Let it alone this year also" (Luke 13:8). Longsuffering is a feature of true love. Love has many levels and so we liken it to fruit. At first it is small on a tree, then it slowly grows and ripens for eating. When love is a ripe fruit ready for eating, longsuffering subsequently comes, "Slow to wrath has great understanding." (Proverbs 14:29). The church fathers tell us, "If you want to judge your spiritual maturity, measure how quickly you become angry." A person with high spiritual maturity does not become angry or upset quickly. In contrast, a person with low spiritual maturity will anger quickly, lose their temper, or take a long time to reconcile with others due to their ego. The golden words that Jesus shares in Matthew 7:12 and Luke 6:31, "Whatever you want men to do to you, do also to them." If we want people to be patient, then we must also be patient with them.

When you stand before God, naked, showing all your weaknesses and sins, pleading for God's mercy and forgiveness, you will see how much longsuffering God has for us. Compare what God does for us and what we do for others. How much does God wait for us, bear with us, encourage us to repent, and forgive us when we ask for His mercy. "The LORD is merciful and gracious, slow to anger, and abounding in mercy." (Psalm 103:8) Also, "He who is slow to anger is better than the mighty, and he who rules his spirit than he who takes a city." (Proverbs 16:32). "As the elect of God, holy and beloved, put on tender mercies, kindness, humility, meekness, longsuffering." (Colossians 3:12)

Many weak people around us require someone to bear with them and help them along their path. Homes and marriages may not be ruined if husbands and wives bear with one another. Think of someone whom you love very much and how you overlook their mistakes and find excuses for them, and even forget their mistakes because "Love bears all things, believes all things, hopes all things, endures all things." (1 Corinthians 13:7). It is for this reason – to invite the work of the Holy Spirit – that the church includes an introduction to the Morning Prayer: "I, therefore, the prisoner of the Lord, beseech you to walk worthy of the calling with which you were called, with all lowliness and gentleness, with longsuffering, bearing with one another in love." (Ephesians 4:1). The person who is slow to anger, suffers long and is calm from within can, "Comfort the fainthearted, uphold the weak, be patient with all." (1 Thessalonians 5:14)

And now for some practical tips on how we can strive to work with the Holy Spirit to produce the fruit of longsuffering:

1. Be the image of God: the Lord is merciful and gracious, slow to anger and abounding in mercy (Psalm 103:8).

2. Bear with sufferings and tribulations: suffering and tribulation all end in salvation, "If indeed we suffer with Him, that we may also be glorified together." (Romans 8:17).

3. Find the connection between love and bearing: practice bearing with others as every challenge is a new opportunity for growth.

4. Always give thanks: the more we thank God, the more we have longsuffering.

5. Remember the heroes of faith: those who strove to reach a life of righteousness just as St. Paul says, "I have fought the good fight, I have finished the race, I have kept the faith. Finally, there is laid up for me the crown of righteousness." (2 Timothy 4:7).

6. Be steadfast in the Lord: satanic wars are many, but be steadfast in the vine and a strong branch through

obedience, keeping His commandments and the means of grace.

7. Don't be selfish: the Lord teaches us to deny ourselves, "Let him deny himself, and take up his cross, and follow Me." (Matthew 16:24).

8. Serve with patience: "We give no offense in anything, that our ministry may not be blamed but in all things we commend ourselves as ministers of God: in much patience, in tribulations, in needs, in distresses." (2 Corinthians 6:3).

Longsuffering will allow us to keep our ultimate goal clear in our mind until our last breath: to be with Christ and inherit the Kingdom of God. For this reason St. Paul praises the Church

MANY WEAK PEOPLE AROUND US REQUIRE SOMEONE TO BEAR WITH THEM AND HELP THEM ALONG THEIR PATH.

of Thessalonica because they bore with persecution, "So that we ourselves boast of you among the churches of God for your patience and faith in all your persecutions and tribulations that you endure." (2 Thessalonians 1:4).

Bearing the Fruits of the Holy Spirit - Kindness

Sometimes we get caught up in the idea that we can't stop a particular sin or weakness in our lives. We become enslaved and bound by evil habits. St. Macarius' 4th homily, "God's patience and His great kindness" speaks of the kindness we should endeavour for. "Our good Lord came into our world, healing the blind and paralysed, cured all kinds of diseases, and even raised the dead, where the body had a stench and was decayed. He gave hearing to the deaf and cast out demons. How much more will He not convert and change a soul who has repented and asked for God's mercy, who needs His shelter and protection. He will return the soul to a state of joy after releasing it from its lusts. Renewing the mind; changing the soul to a state of healthy mental sight and thoughts of peace instead of blindness, deafness, death, ignorance and apathy. He will bring this soul to a purified state with a balanced and clean heart. If the Lord, with that compassion over decayed bodies and with such a kind heart, gave everyone according to their needs, how much more does He do for the immortal, imperishable, incorruptible soul, labouring under the disease of ignorance, wickedness and unbelief?"

Kindness is perhaps the most challenging fruit to attain from the Holy Spirit. St. Paul wrote extensively about kindness because he experienced it directly from God, "Therefore, as the elect of God, holy and beloved, put on tender mercies, kindness, humility, meekness, longsuffering." (Colossians 3:12). And "But when the kindness and the love of God our Saviour toward man appeared" (Titus 3:4). A kind person treats all people with kindness, follows God's commandments, and takes care of all things. If we allow the Holy Spirit to control our life, He will teach us kindness and compassion, and how to forgive just as God forgives. Just as Christ won the hearts of many, even the hard-hearted, through the gentleness He provides: "Or do you despise the riches of His goodness, forbearance, and longsuffering, not knowing that the goodness of God leads you to repentance?" (Romans 2:4).

God's characteristic kindness takes the human soul to the heights, treats it with gentleness, and flatters it, "Therefore, behold, I will allure her, Will bring her into the wilderness, And speak comfort to her." (Hosea 2:14). Kindness is a mixture of all the Bible's virtues blended together. It is the fruit of the life of gentleness, tenderness, cheerfulness, meekness, humility and love. It is the opposite of harshness, violence, cruelty, and arrogance, and since it is the fruit of the Spirit, humankind can attain it through the Holy Spirit.

IF WE ALLOW THE HOLY SPIRIT TO CONTROL OUR LIFE, HE WILL TEACH US KINDNESS AND COMPASSION, AND HOW TO FORGIVE JUST AS GOD FORGIVES.

Spiritual life is not only one of prayer, fasting and going to church. If I alienate myself from others, I cannot be kind to them, then I am pretending to be a Christian.

Consider the outstanding example of kindness in the Parable of the Prodigal Son. When the younger son returned, the father treated him with love and acceptance. He also dealt wisely with his older son, reassuring him of his continued love. Both sons wronged the father in different ways. The younger son did terrible things, but he took him in, embraced him, washed him, put new clothes on him and treated him with gentleness. The older son was cruel to his brother in his judgement of him, but the father embraced him too and soothed him with gentle words of assurance. When our heart is kind, we will find that we do not reproach others or use harsh words to judge them. St. Peter, after he denied Christ, how our Lord sought him at the lake. He did not reproach him but asked him, "Simon, do you love Me?" (John 21:15). This is kindness wins the hearts of others.

Filled with the Holy Spirit

We can read how our Lord won Zacchaeus, the Samaritan woman and the woman caught in adultery by using love, gentleness, kindness, and tenderness. It was said of Christ, "He will not quarrel nor cry out, nor will anyone hear His voice in the streets. A bruised reed He will not break, And smoking flax He will not quench." (Matthew 12:19). When Jesus went to Zacchaeus, He did not remind him of his past life and what he did, but He told him amid all the people, "Zacchaeus, make haste and come down, for today I must stay at your house." (Luke 19: 5) When Jesus went to the Samaritan woman, He spoke with kindness and did not remind her of her past. The woman caught in the very act of adultery was trapped by those preparing to stone her, yet she was handled with kindness by our Lord Jesus. He stooped down and wrote on the ground with His finger the sins of her accusers. He said, "Woman, where are those accusers of yours? Has no one condemned you?" She said, "No one, Lord." And Jesus said to her. "Neither do I condemn you; go and sin no more." (John 8:8-11). Why don't we learn these qualities and resemble Christ? Why are we harsh with our words and hard on others by judging them, or showing no mercy? What a difference it makes: rather than using harsh words to reproach someone of their sins, use kindness from the Holy Spirit to help the sinner confess.

Were it not for the mercy of God and His kindness towards us, we would have perished. Our Lord always forgives the sinner and makes excuses for them. Christ made excuses for the exhausted disciples who were with Him in the Garden of Gethsemane and slept saying, "The spirit indeed is willing, but the flesh is weak." (Matthew 26:41). We too should make excuses for others to become gentle and accommodating to the weaknesses of others: "Comfort the faint hearted, uphold the weak, be patient with all." (1 Thessalonians 5:14). This kindness is a fruit of the Holy Spirit, and if we are filled with the Holy Spirit, we share this kindness with those around us.

Bearing the Fruits of the Holy Spirit- Goodness

We are surrounded by stories of how the early Christians were identified by their good actions and the visible grace on their faces. St. Macarius speaks about this in his 5th homily, "The new creation and the eternal home of the Spirit." He says, "There is a huge difference between the Christian person and the person of this world. The inhabitants of the earth are like wheat thrown into the sieve of this earth, sifted by the restless thoughts of this world, tossed without ceasing by waves of earthly matters and lusts and entangled by material thinking. The devils have been given authority to sieve us in the earthly worries of this world. This sieve aims to break up God's commandments just like the wheat in the sieve is stirred by the sifter, moving from side to side, colliding within the sieve. The chief of evil catches all people, shaking them, stirring them up, provoking them, striking them with evil, earthly, vain lusts, earthly bound. As Jesus said in Luke 22:31, "Indeed, Satan has asked for you, that he may sift you as wheat, But I have prayed for you, that your faith should not fail." The whole of humanity shakes in this sieve and this leads them into restless, anxious thoughts, lusts of the world, earthly affairs, the pleasure of the flesh and fears that can drown us completely."

Absolute goodness is only the nature of God, but as humans, we have the fruit of goodness if we are connected to God. God's goodness is bestowed on the righteous and unrighteous, upon the worthy and unworthy. King David's Psalm tells us, "The LORD is good; His mercy is everlasting." (Psalm 100:5). In the Second Hoas of the Midnight Praises, "Give thanks to the Lord for He is good! For His mercy endures forever." (Psalm 136:1). How are Christians different from the rest of humanity? The distinguishing features are not the external appearances such as a cross around our neck or on our wrist, but rather their heart, mind and way of thinking. True Christians see eternal good in the world because they have received the Holy Spirit and His fellowship. Their mind and soul have the peace of Christ and the love of the Spirit.

The fruit of goodness may be displayed in different ways:

1. The work of love: to care about others in need, feed the poor, give clothes to those without, help the sick, mourn with the sad, and look after the spiritual and physical needs

of others. This unconditional love follows in the footsteps of Christ: "Come, you who are blessed by my Father; inherit the kingdom prepared for you from the foundation of the world, For I was hungry and you gave Me food, I was thirsty and you gave Me drink, I was a stranger and you took Me in, I was naked and you clothed Me, I was sick and you visited Me, I was in prison and you came to Me." (Matthew 25:34-36).

2. Integrity: fleeing from sin and being virtuous. Pope Shenouda taught that there are two aspects to goodness and fleeing from sin: what we should not do, and what we should do. We should not sin, and not have any other gods but Him as specified in the Ten Commandments. In his Epistle to the Hebrews, St. Paul says, "You have not yet resisted to bloodshed, striving against sin." (Hebrews 12:4). The struggle against sin is a good deed. In addition, what we should be doing is imitating the New Testament Beatitudes in the Gospel of Matthew: blessed are the poor in spirit, blessed are the meek, blessed are the merciful, blessed are the pure in heart, blessed are the peacemakers and so on. Pope Shenouda continues by saying, "You shall love the LORD your God with all your heart, with all your soul, with all your strength, and with all your mind." (Luke 10: 27).

In Chapter 9 of the Acts of the Apostles, we read the story of Tabitha. She was filled with the fruit of goodness from the Holy Spirit and performed good deeds helping the poor, the widows and the sick. She became very sick and eventually she died, so they sent for St. Peter, and showed him all the clothes that Tabitha had made for the poor. St. Peter knelt and prayed, and then raised Tabitha from the dead.

Tabitha's many good deeds for others were rewarded with such a miraculous display of God's glory. If our hearts are filled with goodness from the Holy Spirit, we will do good things for all people – whether Christian or not, whether one colour or another – and our life too will be for the glory of God.

> ❋
> TRUE CHRISTIANS SEE ETERNAL GOOD IN THE WORLD BECAUSE THEY HAVE RECEIVED THE HOLY SPIRIT AND HIS FELLOWSHIP. THEIR MIND AND SOUL HAVE THE PEACE OF CHRIST AND THE LOVE OF THE SPIRIT.

Goodness as a fruit of the Holy Spirit in fact has a double meaning. The act of the Holy Spirit in the human heart, and the work of the human with the Holy Spirit to create the fruit of Goodness. It is two-pronged because the Holy Spirit works in our heart, and we work with the Holy Spirit. St. Mark the Hermit said, "Any believer who lives according to the commandments and has a successful spiritual life, must believe that the power to follow the commandments is given by the Holy Spirit. The Holy Spirit was received in the Sacrament of Confirmation, after Baptism, and this is the source of every good deed and every virtue from inside and outside." Our human nature is wired to be self-centred rather than good to others, so unless we fill our heart with the Holy Spirit, we will never be capable of goodness. We will have no fruits if we refuse to cooperate with the Holy Spirit. With this mind, let us reflect on the prayer of St. Augustine, "If there is anything good in me,

You are the source of it. The good in me is Your good, and from You I accept it."

Bearing the Fruits of the Holy Spirit -Faithfulness

St. Paul teaches us to faithfully strive in this life saying, "For we know that if our earthly house, this tent, is destroyed, we have a building from God, a house not made with hands, eternal in the heavens." (2 Corinthians 5:1). If the house of our earthly body is destroyed, we must strive with every virtue to ensure we are not exposed, "If indeed, having been clothed, we shall not be found naked." (2 Corinthians 5:3). Naked refers to separation from the Holy Spirit; as Christians, we should not be afraid when we leave this body because by the power and strength of the Holy Spirit within us, we enter an eternal, heavenly and incorruptible house. Endeavouring with faithful diligence allows us to acquire that garment here and now, such that we will never be found naked.

The word 'faith' in Arabic – which our parents may use – differs slightly from the English 'faithfulness.' So, to avoid any confusion let us consider the original word in Greek: 'pistis' which has two meanings. The first denotes truth, honesty and authenticity, and the second is trust and dependence. As a gift of the Holy Spirit, it equates to trust and dependence on God's power. Faith is the foundation of our relationship with God; it is an act of our will – a purposeful decision – to trust in Him. There are many verses we have about this: "But without faith it is impossible to please Him." (Hebrews 11:6). "Examine yourself as to whether you are in the faith." (2 Corinthians 13:5). "And this is the victory that has overcome the world - our faith." (1 John 5:4). "And now abide faith, hope, love, these three; but the greatest of these is love." (1 Corinthians 13:13)

Let us enjoy the New Testament's great personalities to understand the theory and practice of faith.

1. Believing in the promises of God:

I. St. Mary: it was said of her, "Blessed is she who believed, for there will be a fulfillment of those things which were told her from the Lord." (Luke 1:45). She was blessed because she believed all that was said to her by the Angel Gabriel. Do we believe all that God has said to us?

II. The Shepherds: "Do not be afraid, for behold, I bring you good tidings of great joy which will be to all people... Let us now go to Bethlehem and see this thing that has come to pass, which the Lord has made known to us." (Luke 2:10, 15).

III. Simeon the Elder: "This man was just and devout, waiting for the Consolation of Israel, and the Holy Spirit was upon him. And it had been revealed to him by the Holy Spirit that he would not see death before he had seen the Lord's Christ." (Luke 2:25-26). Indeed, Simeon carried the Lord Jesus in his arms just as he was promised.

2. Act on your belief: when Christ saw the actions of the four friends that carried their paralysed friend through the ceiling to reach Him and be healed, He told the paralysed man, "Son, your sins are forgiven you." (Mark 2:5). True faith makes us go beyond standard solutions, and even risk danger, to meet God.

3. Believe instantly rather than calculate the cost: to Matthew the tax collector, Christ said, "Follow Me." (Matthew 9:9) and he quickly left everything, arose and followed Him. Imagine what he saw in Jesus that day to abandon his life based on Christ's two words. No doubt Matthew was an expert at complex mathematical calculations, but dealing with God's plans, language, and wisdom does not need this from us.

4. Have confidence in the unseen: faith is imperceptible to our five senses but is made manifest through actions:

I. The Centurion: had extraordinary confidence when he said to Christ, "Lord, do not trouble Yourself, for I am not worthy that You should enter under my roof. Therefore I did not even think myself worthy to come to You. But say the word, and my servant will be healed." (Luke 7:6-7). His faith did not require Jesus to come anywhere near his servant to heal him. Compare this with our faith: despite going to church, listening to sermons or posting bible verses on our social media, the moment we face a small trial our faith evaporates.

ENDEAVOURING WITH FAITHFUL DILIGENCE ALLOWS US TO ACQUIRE THAT GARMENT HERE AND NOW, SUCH THAT WE WILL NEVER BE FOUND NAKED.

II. The woman who was bleeding for many years: her whole livelihood was wasted on physicians who could not help her, so she "Came from behind and touched the border of His garment. And immediately her flow of blood stopped." (Luke 8:44). Faith that simply touching the hem of Jesus' garment is all she needed to be healed.

III. Bartimaeus the blind man: sitting by the roadside begging, he heard the Lord was passing by and cried out, "Son of David, have mercy on me." (Mark 10:46). Those around him scolded him for such a racket but he persisted. Ultimately the Lord Jesus said, "Go your way, your faith has made you well." (Mark 10: 52). We see here two sides of the coin: one is faith with no solution, so we start by calling out loudly and asking for God's mercy. The other is complete trust that God is the only one who can fix our problem, despite all the noise and discouragement we may receive from others.

IV. The Canaanite woman: when she called out to Christ, He said to her, "It is not good to take the children's bread and throw it to the little dogs." (Matthew 15:26) to which she replied, "Yes, Lord, yet even the little dogs eat the crumbs which fall from their masters' table." (Matthew 15:27). He said to her, "O woman, great is your faith!" (Matthew 15:28). She did not defend or resist, nor was she arrogant, nor did she object. Instead she said, 'Yes, I am a Gentile, I am cursed; but this does not prevent her from taking crumbs to give to my daughter to be healed. Whenever we grovel before Him, we obtain our cure.

V. Demon-possessed man: this man's father informed Jesus that his son was demon-possessed and was not cured by His disciples. Jesus said, "O faithless generation, how long shall I be with you? How long shall I bear with you? Bring him here to Me." The man said, "If You can do anything, have compassion on us and help us." Jesus said to the father, "If you can believe, all things are possible to him who believes." Immediately the child's father cried out and said with tears, "Lord, I believe; help my unbelief!" (Mark 9:17-25). What a beautiful picture of faith this is. He was given a promise to which he became attached, crying out with tears of helplessness and weeping.

The terms and conditions of faith are not given to us in fine print to be hidden, but instead very loudly proclaimed: "Have faith in God. For assuredly, I say to you, whoever says to this mountain, 'Be removed and be cast into the sea,' and does not doubt in his heart, but believes that those things he says will be done, he will have whatever he says. Therefore, I say to you, whatever things you ask when you pray, believe that you receive them, and you will have them." (Mark 11:23-24). The conditions are therefore:

1. Do not doubt in your heart.

2. Whatever things you ask in prayer, have faith that you will receive it.

3. Whenever you stand praying, be in a state of forgiveness.

Faith through the Holy Spirit is trusting in every word and every promise written in the Bible. Do not doubt, but take it with confidence, as the Lord said, "Heaven and earth will pass away, but My words will by no means pass away." (Luke 21:33).

Bearing the Fruits of the Holy Spirit -Gentleness

In the first book of Kings, we read about the prophet Elijah's unique experience. He opposed the prophets of Baal, whom Jezebel (wife of King Ahab) followed. Elijah said in his golden famous words, "How long will you falter between two opinions? If the LORD is God, follow Him; but if Baal, follow him." (1 Kings 18:21). Not surprisingly, Elijah's offering was accepted by God, and the offerings of Baal were rejected.

The Hebrew word for gentleness comes from bowing, which is humility. After this great victory, Elijah feared Jezebel and fled, but the beauty of our Lord is that He does not leave His people but continues to support them. God sent him food and drink, and not only that, but God Himself appeared to Elijah the Prophet and spoke to him. God asked him, "What are you doing here, Elijah?" Elijah replied, "I have been very zealous for the LORD God of hosts; for the children of Israel have forsaken Your covenant, torn down Your altars, and killed Your prophets with the sword. I alone am left; and they seek to take my life." Then the Lord said, "Go out, and stand on the mountain before the Lord." And behold, the Lord passed by, and a great and strong wind tore into the mountains and broke the rocks in pieces before the Lord, but the Lord was not in the wind; and after the wind, an earthquake, but the Lord was not in the earthquake; and after the earthquake, a fire, but the Lord was not in the fire; and after the fire, a still small voice. So it was, when Elijah heard it, that he wrapped his face in his mantle and went out and stood in the entrance of the cave. Suddenly a voice came to him, and said, "What are you doing here, Elijah?" (1 Kings 19:9-13).

To describe a gentle person, we may use such words as quiet, peaceful, cheerful, slow to anger, or softly spoken. Remember that self-control is a sign of spiritual maturity: "Brethren, if a man is overtaken in any trespass, you who are spiritual restore such a one in a spirit of gentleness, considering yourself lest you also be tempted." (Galatians 6:1). Gentleness is one of the characteristics of Jesus, "Learn from Me, for I am gentle and lowly in heart." (Matthew 11:29). Jesus was the epitome of humility, gentleness and mercy toward even those who despised him. Consider how Jesus dealt with the Samaritan woman – he did not scrutinise her weaknesses or sins, but He saw that she had a beautiful heart full of love. The same was true for the sinner woman who washed His feet with her tears. He told her that her sins were forgiven. This is the spirit that Jesus wants us to have: a humble heart, respecting and appreciating others, and not being too hard on them.

A gentle person can tolerate others without grumbling, not because of their ability but through the power of the Holy Spirit within them. "A soft answer turns away wrath" (Proverbs 15:1). St. Isaac says, "It is easy to move a mountain, but not easy to stir a gentle person from their gentleness." The gentle soul does not analyse others; or how they think, act, look and feel. The gentle soul feels ashamed to examine others, is transparent, straightforward, calm, and is not defensive even if oppressed. St. Athanasius tells us St. Anthony is the perfect example of this: "Because of his gentleness, all his children in monkhood became gentle. The desert they lived in is called 'The Land of Gentleness.'"

Gentleness is a loveable characteristic of God that He wants all His children to have. "The beauty of a gentle and quiet spirit, which is very precious in God's sight." (1 Peter 3:4). It may manifest in our daily actions such as shopping, driving, working, dealing with others in humility and accepting the word of God, in contrast to the angry person who is always triggered. Gentleness is a living testimonial to God; when we see it in others, it gives glory to God and His work. The first blessing in St. Matthew's Beatitudes is, "Blessed are the meek; for they shall inherit the earth." (Matthew 5:5). St. Paul said in Colossians, "Therefore, as the elect of God, holy and beloved, put on tender mercies, kindness, humility, meekness." (Colossians 3:12)

Anba Isidore, the monk of Scetis helped St. Moses the Strong repent, and always hosted the disobedient monks and treated them with patience and kindness until they

GENTLENESS IS A LOVEABLE CHARACTERISTIC OF GOD THAT HE WANTS ALL HIS CHILDREN TO HAVE.

repented. When asked why the demons feared him, he replied, "Because I have never been angry." St. Agathon said, "The angry man, even if he raises the dead to life, is not accepted by God, in fact, no one accepts him." Who is responsible for the gentleness in us? Surely the Holy Spirit will give us this fruit if we submit and allow it to work within us.

Next time you are in the church, examine the icons around you, for example of the Virgin Mary or St. George. There is an exudation of gentleness and meekness from even the icons of those who please the Lord with their good deeds. One of the early church fathers, Father Jacob, said, "The gentle person on earth will be an angel in heaven." Open your heart, discipline yourself to learn and remove all arrogance to trust in the Spirit. "Receive with meekness the implanted word, which is able to save your souls." (James 1:21).

Bearing the Fruits of the Holy Spirit- Selfcontrol

The final fruit of the Holy Spirit is self-control. In St. Macarius' 7th homily, "Christ's love and His kindness toward mankind," we contemplate the amazing opportunity we have if we allow the Holy Spirit into our life. "Imagine entering the royal palace of a well-known king, seeing portraits, works of art, treasures and luxurious furniture. The king then invites you to sit at the table with him. The table is furnished with expensive gold utensils and delicious food and drink. After looking at all these things in great joy and delight, you are thrown out to a place of great contrast to this, a very dirty palace. Or imagine a beautiful young lady, superior in beauty, intelligence and wealth, who marries a poor, lowly, ugly man dressed in rags. She then removes his old clothes and replaces them with royal clothes, puts a crown on his head and then enters into union with him through marriage. In amazement and astonishment, the poor man says, 'I, the miserable, poor, ugly man, have such a wife given to me?' This is what God does with the wretched, poor person. He has given them a taste of the delicious, heavenly food from the other world. He has shown them the unspeakable royal glories and the beauties of the heavenly treasures, the eternal life. When one compares these spiritual glories to the affairs of this world, one will cast away those unworthy things and turn their eyes, gazing towards the heavenly treasures. Because God is love, He has given man to obtain the heavenly, divine fire of Christ, through which man feels rested and rejoices with exultation and remains there always. This fire is the fire of the Holy Spirit."

Self-control requires total submission to the Holy Spirit, of our mind, emotions and actions. St. Paul teaches, "And everyone who competes for the prize is temperate in all things." (1 Corinthians 9:25) and similarly in Titus, "For a bishop must be blameless, as a steward of God, not self-willed, not quick-tempered, not given to wine, not violent, not greedy for money, but hospitable, a lover of what is good, sober-minded just, Holy, Self-Controlled." (Titus 1:7-8). St. John of Kronstadt from our sister Russian Orthodox Church said, "This fruit, self-control, is vital in dealing with others. To control others, you must first control yourself, and in order to teach others, you must first acquire knowledge. If I do not know how to control myself and do not have the spirit of gentleness, holiness, love and righteousness, then I am an invalid mastermind."

St. Peter was considered impulsive before receiving the grace of self-control and teaches us from his experience "Giving all diligence, add to your faith virtue, to virtue knowledge, to knowledge self-control, to self-control perseverance. For if these things are yours and abound, you will be neither barren nor unfruitful in the knowledge of our Lord Jesus Christ." (2 Peter 1:5-8). Self-control belongs to the wise and must be exerted on every desire of the flesh which enslaves us: sexual desire, gluttony, clothes, money and any other worldly temptations. That is why believers are called to be spiritual, not carnal creatures. "We are debtors – not to the flesh, to live according to the flesh. For if you live according to the flesh you will die; but if by the Spirit you put to death the deeds of the body, you will live." (Romans 8:12-13).

Reflect on your own experience: are there any situations you regretted not exercising self-control? Perhaps you should not have opened your mouth so quickly in retaliation or given your harsh opinion to that unfortunate person. In the Deuterocanonical Book of Wisdom of Joshua, the Son of Sirach 18:30, we read, "Go not after your lusts, but turn away from your own will. If you give to your soul her desires, she will make you a joy to your enemies." Equally St. Paul teaches in Romans, "Make no provision for the flesh, to fulfill its lusts." (Romans 13:14), and again in Galatians; "I say then: Walk in the Spirit, and you shall not fulfill the lust of the flesh." (Galatians 5:16).

When the Catholic epistle is read during the Holy Liturgy, we conclude with the words from the First epistle of St. John, "Do not love the world or the things in the world. If anyone loves the world,

SELF-CONTROL REQUIRES TOTAL SUBMISSION TO THE HOLY SPIRIT, OF OUR MIND, EMOTIONS AND ACTIONS.

the love of the Father is not in him. For all that is in the world – the lust of the flesh, the lust of the eyes, and the pride of life – is not of the Father but is of the world." (1 John 2:15). These three temptations that he lists do not cease to fight us, occupy us, disrupt us and distract us throughout our life. St. Cyril of Jerusalem said, "Let us all hasten, by the grace of God, to the race of purity, young and old, to praise the name of Christ, far from gluttony. We do not deny the glory of chastity; it is an angelic crown, a virtue that transcends the human being."

Disciplining the body is a great virtue that comforts the mind, the eyes, the tongue, and all the senses. Let us keep our eyes on the goal of receiving fruit from self-control from the Holy Spirit, "But I discipline my body and bring it into subjection… lest I myself should become disqualified." (1 Corinthians 9:27).

The True Christian is Filled with the Spirit

St. Macarius' 16th homily, "You are invited to be above all tribulations," speaks of the key elements of a spiritual life. "God created us in a state of innocence, but evil came due to free will. The Creator made all angels and humans in a state of innocence and perfectly simple. The fact that some of them have turned to evil was an after-effect of free will. As for us, evil works powerfully, making itself tangible and inspiring all evil desires. But evil does not mingle with us. It is like the wheat and the tares; both are mixed together, growing in the same field, yet having their own entity." St. Macarius also gives us an example of the mingling of sin with the soul: "The spring of water comes as clear water, even though there is mud at the bottom of the spring. If someone stirs the mud, the whole spring becomes murky. Likewise, when the soul is aroused, it becomes defiled; the soul is mixed with evil and becomes one [with it], as in fornication and adultery."

St Macarius compares our relationship with the Holy Spirit to a wife who becomes one with her husband in matrimony. Their bond is mighty but can be broken if one spouse dies and the other lives. This is like the fellowship of the Holy Spirit with the soul; they become one spirit, "But he who is joined to the Lord is one spirit with Him." (1 Corinthians 6:17). This unity happens when we are filled with the Holy Spirit and, as St Macarius says, are "swallowed up in grace."

Although we may have tasted God, we are still subject to the influences of the enemy due to our lack of spiritual experience in our relationship with Him. Just like the widow is separated from her husband by death, we may lose our communion with the Holy Spirit by falling into sin. In contrast, when we endure tribulations, we gain spiritual experience with God and knowing that it is for our benefit we should not despair. If someone is rich in grace, although they may battle their desires and lusts, they should have constant hope in God who will wither and dry out any remaining evil. Indeed, evil is real because it resides and works in our hearts with wicked and unclean thoughts. Most commonly it causes us not to pray in purity and concentration, and draws our minds into slavery in this world, affecting our entire body and soul. Instead, we should persist with eagerness and awe in our hearts for

The True Christian is Filled with the Spirit

God's grace. This grace wakes us up to strive day and night without ceasing and changes our heart.

A true Christian is from another world; they are the children of the heavenly Adam, a new race, children of the Holy Spirit and the luminous brothers of Christ. As Jesus said of them in His prayer, "They are not of this world." (John 17:16). Unlike those who heap up earthly treasures, those who make heavenly riches the object of their work, bring joy and happiness to the saints and angels; and when they depart from this world, they will rejoice with the Lord in heaven. That is the importance of sobriety and spiritual discernment so that our hearts do not get attached to earthly things.

An important step is to distinguish between the dwelling and the filling of the Holy Spirit. In the Sacrament of Confirmation, after Baptism, we receive the dwelling of the Holy Spirit. It is like a cup to which we add a few drops of water: as an optimist we can't say it is empty, but it is certainly not full. It can only be full when it is filled to the brim, which is entirely different to a few drops. This is the filling of the Holy Spirit. The Church Fathers agree that our spiritual works are due to being filled with the Holy Spirit. When we read the Bible, it is not an academic analysis of every verse, but rather to simply be filled with the Spirit. Our fathers and mothers, the saints, aimed to benefit from the Holy Spirit by spending long hours with the Holy Bible, eating and being nourished by the words of God. Similarly, when we attend Mass and have Holy Communion, we again do so to be filled.

Consider the Parable of the Five Wise and Five Foolish Virgins, which the Church puts before us daily in the

Filled with the Holy Spirit

Midnight Prayer of the Agpeya. They all had vessels, but at the end of the parable, we see that the vessels of the five wise virgins were filled with oil – representing the Holy Spirit – while the vessels of the five foolish virgins did not. The vessels are a symbol of the heart; those filled with the Holy Spirit have power, light, love, peace, and joy and have the fruits of the Holy Spirit. We can therefore divide people into two groups: wise and foolish. The wise person's goal is to be filled with the Holy Spirit, but the foolish one will not benefit. "[Though I] give my body to be burned, but have no love, it profits me nothing." (1 Corinthians 13:3).

The word of God is the first step toward being filled with the Holy Spirit. "The words that I speak to you are spirit, and they are life." (John 6:63). Every time you read the words of God, you eat them; every time you live the words of God, you will be filled with the Holy Spirit without knowing. The saints spiritually extend themselves to be humble and deny themselves because the Holy Spirit loves to see a broken, contrite and humble heart. Can you or I truly lose our ego, dignity and perhaps our money, in order to be flooded with the presence of the Holy Spirit? "Out of his heart will flow rivers of living water." (John 7:38). Every time we accomplish God's commandment in the Bible, we will be filled with the Holy Spirit. "You are the temple of God and that the Spirit of God dwells in you." (1 Corinthians 3:16). The lives of the Saints were not smooth; they suffered much, but they knew that in the end, they would be filled with the Holy Spirit.

The Holy Spirit fills and comforts us every time we stand to pray. When we pray for others, for repentance or for grace, the Holy Spirit fills us and enlightens us. St. Bishoy

The True Christian is Filled with the Spirit

prayed a lot, which is why he was the only one who recognised the Lord Jesus on the road up the mountain. He was filled with the Holy Spirit, and he had much oil in his lamp. He strived as the Lord said, "Strive to enter through the narrow gate." (Luke 13:24) We learn from him that this requires determination, awareness, a strong will, open-mindedness and a grand vision open to heaven. Whenever we strive to reach the narrow gate through fasting, prayer, or tribulations, our heart shines with grace. However, the evil one does not like seeing that and therefore fights us. If we find hatred, grudges or wrath in our hearts, we will know we are not yet full.

Complaining and grumbling subdues the Holy Spirit within us. Instead, give abundant thanks and gratitude to the Lord, not only with your lips but also from your heart. Inner gratitude is essential as the Lord said, "These people draw near to Me with their mouth, and honour Me with their lips, But their heart is far from Me." (Matthew 15:8). Each time we give thanks to God with deep gratitude, He fills us with the Holy Spirit.

Our Church gives us this reading in the Midnight prayer each night, "Walk while you have the light, lest darkness overtake you." (John 12:35). The Church wants her children to be filled with the Holy Spirit, enlightened and strong, to produce a powerful Church. We can be witnesses to our

> ❋
> A TRUE CHRISTIAN IS FROM ANOTHER WORLD; THEY ARE THE CHILDREN OF THE HEAVENLY ADAM, A NEW RACE, CHILDREN OF THE HOLY SPIRIT AND THE LUMINOUS BROTHERS OF CHRIST.

Lord and be joyful in this task; have true love without hypocrisy, abounding in meekness, gentleness and long suffering. The Holy Spirit is the Spirit of every good gift in us and the reason to go to church; from inside we will see Jesus, and from outside others will see Jesus in us.

Don't Quench the Holy Spirit

St. Gregory the Theologian said these powerful words about the Holy Spirit, on which we can meditate: "He is called the Spirit of God, the Spirit of Christ, the mind of Christ, the Spirit of the Lord, and Himself the Lord, the Spirit of adoption, of truth, of liberty; the Spirit of wisdom, of understanding, of counsel, of might, of knowledge, of Godliness, of the fear of God. For He is the maker of all these, filling all with His essence, containing all things, filling the world in His essence, yet incapable of being comprehended in His power by the world; good, upright, princely, by nature not by adoption; sanctifying, not sanctified; measuring, not measured; shared, not sharing; filling, not filled; containing, not contained; inherited, glorified, reckoned with the Father and the Son; held out as a threat; the Finger of God; fire like God; to manifest, as I take it, His consubstantiality"

A sailing ship cannot move without wind, even if it has all the instruments and navigation. Similarly, without the grace of the Holy Spirit, we cannot pass through the sea of this life to cross over to the shore of salvation and eternal life. Let us examine how we ignite the grace of the Holy Spirit:

1. Subject yourself and submit to God: "The Holy Spirit whom God has given to those who obey Him." (Acts 5:32). We cannot be filled unless we are obedient to God, even though there is often some resistance at first.

2. Cleanse the heart from evil thoughts: we can all agree that darkness does not exist in the light; the devil Beelzebub cannot reside near God. St. John Chrysostom said, "Can we be filled with the Holy Spirit? Yes, we definitely can. When we cleanse our souls from lies, anger, uncleanliness, and greed, and when we acquire kindness, mercy and forgiveness, we are truly worthy of Him. So then, what prevents the Holy Spirit from coming close to us and enlightening us? He will not only come to us but will fill our hearts so that it is not difficult to accomplish the path of virtues."

3. Prayer: with faith, with longing, with strength, with feeling, with honesty, with humility, with meekness, with a contrite heart, with fervour and with self-denial. "If you then, being evil, know how to give good gifts to your children, how much more will your heavenly Father give the Holy Spirit to those who ask Him." (Luke 11:13).

St. Anthony, in his 8th Homily said, "Lift your thoughts to heaven, day and night, and the Holy Spirit will be given to you." St. John Chrysostom said, "Whoever chants Psalms day and night, fills their soul with the Spirit."

4. The Word of God: as St. John Chrysostom said, "We must constantly kindle within us the fire of the Holy Spirit with the Word of God, divine matters and spiritual works."

In the same way we remind ourselves of what we should do to gain the Holy Spirit, so too we should review things we should avoid. The bible lists these four things:

1. Do not quench the Spirit (1 Thessalonians 5:19).

2. Do not grieve the Spirit (Ephesians 4:30).

3. Do not resist the Spirit (Acts 7:51).

4. Do not blaspheme the Spirit (Matthew 12:31).

The Holy Spirit is quenched when we are lazy and fail to strive in our spiritual life. The Holy Spirit is grieved when we fall into sin, stay in sin, and make no effort to escape it. Common obstacles include:

> ✳
> WITHOUT THE GRACE OF THE HOLY SPIRIT, WE CANNOT PASS THROUGH THE SEA OF THIS LIFE TO CROSS OVER TO THE SHORE OF SALVATION AND ETERNAL LIFE.

1. Living in sin and impurity: St. Anthony said, "This Spirit doesn't dwell in any soul. It dwells only in those completely purified from their lusts because the Holy Spirit cannot enter an unclean soul." When the soul becomes defiled

by sin, this will cause the Holy Spirit to grieve. David the Prophet said, "If I regard iniquity in my heart, The Lord will not hear." (Psalm 66:18).

2. Love of the world: if we give our heart to the world, we depend on the world and are ruled by things of the world: money, lust and fame. St. John Chrysostom said, "The world has darkness, thick fog and dark clouds, but the conscientious, intelligent and wise, spiritual person must walk amid this darkness, with the light and the lamp of the grace of the Holy Spirit within them."

3. The sin of pride: some refer to this as the mother of all sins. Many saints have given us their wisdom to fight pride and obtain humility. St. Macarius said, "Anyone who does not abide in humility, surrenders themself to Satan and is stripped of the divine grace that was previously given to them. They will be tempted with many tribulations. Only then will they know their reality; that they are naked and mischievous."

4. Lack of mercy: when our heart has no mercy on others, lacks forgiveness and has no pity for our brothers and sisters, we cannot be filled.

5. Unsanctified prayer: pride or self-interest may overtake us if we go into our prayer room and ask for our own will be done, not His. "You ask and do not receive, because you ask amiss, that you may spend it on your pleasures." (James 4:3)

Hard is the heart of the person who grieves the Holy Spirit. Despite all this, God still tries to bring us back to Him. The Holy Spirit convicts us of sin, guides us, and has no pleasure in the sinner's death. Hence, the Holy Spirit works on leading the sinner to repentance until they accept the Holy Spirit. We continually pray that God guides us and continues His works to fill us with His Holy Spirit and never allow us to grieve His Spirit.

Be Filled with the Spirit

In the Old Testament, when evil increased among the children of God before the flood, the Lord said, "My Spirit shall not strive with man forever, for he is indeed flesh." (Genesis 6:3). Whenever God's men turned away from Him, it was followed by the Spirit of God departing from them. One such man was King Saul, the first king of Israel, "The Spirit of the LORD departed from Saul" (1 Samuel 16:14). Another was King David when he fell into sin with Bathsheba, Nathan the prophet was sent to scold him "Why have you despised the commandment of the LORD, to do evil in His sight?" (2 Samuel 12:9). David cried out saying, "Do not cast me away from Your presence, And do not take Your Holy Spirit from me," (Psalm 51:11) because he saw the Spirit of God departing from Saul.

In the New Testament, the situation is entirely different. If we turn away from God, the Holy Spirit never leaves us because of the grace which we have received. When we feel our weakness, we return to examine ourselves and live a careful life. The only way we may abandon the Holy Spirit is apostasy – to completely renounce our Christian faith. One of the saints said, "The Spirit that we put on in the Water of Baptism cannot be taken off except through apostasy. With faith we put on the Spirit. With denial of the faith, we take off the Spirit."

God, who gives us the Holy Spirit in the Sacrament of Confirmation, warns us not to quench the Holy Spirit with spiritual apathy. "I know your works, that you are neither cold nor hot. I could wish you were cold or hot. So then, because you are lukewarm, and neither cold nor hot, I will omit you out of My mouth." (Revelation 3:15-16). Truly the Holy Spirit does not leave us in any particular sin, but He shuts off His work in us, much like fire if we throw sand or water on it to extinguish it. Therefore, any sin which takes away purity or holiness, quenches the fire of the Holy Spirit in our heart. St. Macarius the Great said, "The Holy Spirit cannot be quenched; it is a continuous light." However, if we are neglectful and careless in cooperating with the Holy Spirit, then this will quench our reception of the Holy Spirit.

There are several ways we – perhaps unknowingly – refuse the fire of the Holy Spirit in our heart:

1. Associating with ungodly people: following and imitating their ways will immediately quench the Holy Spirit. When St. Peter talked about God rescuing Lot out of Sodom, he said "For that righteous man, dwelling among them, tormented his righteous soul from day to day by seeing and hearing their lawless deeds." (2 St Peter: 2:8).

2. Laziness: this is the biggest enemy of humankind and a significant contributor to quenching the Holy Spirit in our life. It is a gradual decline: we stop praying from the Agpeya, stop praying our prayers, go to sleep without praying, serve without praying, reduce or postpone our Bible reading and so on.

3. Stopping acts of love: the internal flame of the Holy Spirit is again gradually extinguished; we stop helping others, begin to judge, despise, hate, take revenge, lack forgiveness, and have unholy feelings. We try to justify all these wrong actions and feelings to ease our conscience. Our justifications might seem reasonable on the outside, but we have no love deep down. If you notice this in your life, quickly repent and allow the Holy Spirit to work inside you again.

What is the danger of extinguishing the Holy Spirit inside us? The Holy Spirit is the Spirit of wisdom and therefore if we lose Him, we also lose wisdom to discern right from wrong. St. John Chrysostom said, "When a thief enters a house, he turns off the light to obtain his object. Likewise, the devil wants to enter the believer's heart to turn off the light of the Holy Spirit." We begin to doubt the word of God and lose trust in the teachings of the Church. We justify our sins and silence our conscience towards sin. We lose the desire to pray and begin to occupy our minds with other things, such as matters of the world. The devil celebrates at our defeat as we gradually fall into further sin and refuse God. All this because the Holy Spirit has been quenched from within.

Importantly, we must not resist the Holy Spirit which works in us without cancelling our freedom. He leads us to do good but does not force us to do it.

IF WE TURN AWAY FROM GOD, THE HOLY SPIRIT NEVER LEAVES US BECAUSE OF THE GRACE WHICH WE HAVE RECEIVED.

He gives us power but leaves us free to decide whether to use it. For this reason, one of the devil's names in Arabic is 'mu-aned' as he persuasively makes us 'stubborn' against the Spirit. Since the beginning of creation, you can find examples of humankind resisting the Holy Spirit, "They made their hearts like flint, refusing to hear the law and the words which the Lord of hosts had sent by His Spirit through the former prophets." (Zechariah 7:12). Many continue to resist the Holy Spirit, "All day long, I have stretched out My hands to a disobedient and contrary people." (Romans 10:21). Similarly, we must not blaspheme the Holy Spirit, as was done by many kings in the Old Testament, with evil sayings or inappropriate behaviour among people. "Therefore I say to you, every sin and blasphemy will be forgiven men, but the blasphemy against the Spirit will not be forgiven men." (Matthew 12:31). St. Paul speaks of Hymenaeus and Alexander, who blasphemed God for their inappropriate behaviour as believers. He punished them by removing them from the Church, "Of whom are Hymenaeus and Alexander, whom I delivered to Satan that they may learn not to blaspheme." (1 Timothy 1:20).

St. John Chrysostom said, "The Holy Spirit makes us part of God's flock, separates us from the past and prevents us from falling into anything that disappoints the Lord God; Ask your conscience, will this grieve the Holy Spirit?" Likewise, St. Paul says, "Do not grieve the Holy Spirit of God." (Ephesians 4:30). In Greek, 'grieve' means to annoy or cause pain. This happens because of a life of sin: bad character traits, unholy words, devious acts, anger, hatred or unforgiveness will immediately grieve the Holy Spirit because He is the Spirit of enlightenment, knowledge and truth. If we realise we have grieved the Spirit, we may feel the internal pain of failure or loss, which encourages us to return.

May God grant us always to be filled with the Holy Spirit, be in communion with the Holy Spirit, and live with the power of the Holy Spirit.

To God is due all glory, forever and ever. Amen.

Scan the QR code to go to our website where you will find

- Book reviews

- Great deals

- Our full library of books

www.ingramcontent.com/pod-product-compliance
Lightning Source LLC
Chambersburg PA
CBHW022110090426
42743CB00008B/793